THE ALCHEMICAL MANDALA

'Squaring the Circle'
Emblem 25 from Michael Maier's
Atalanta Fugiens

THE ALCHEMICAL MANDALA

A Survey of the Mandala in the Western Esoteric Traditions

By Adam McLean

Phanes Press

For further books on alchemy and the Hermetic tradition,
write for a free catalogue or visit our website:

PHANES PRESS, INC.
PO Box 6114
Grand Rapids, MI 49516
www.phanes.com

Second edition

9 8 7 6 5 4 3 2 1
Printed in the United States of America
♾ This edition is printed on acid-free paper
that meets the American National Standards Institute Z39.48 Standard.

Book design by David Fideler.
Cover design by Tracy Therian Olmsted.

Library of Congress Cataloging-in-Publication Data
McLean, Adam.
The alchemical mandala : a survey of the mandala in the Western esoteric traditions / by Adam McLean.
p. cm.
ISBN 1-890482-95-1 (alk. paper)
1. Mandala—Miscellanea. 2. Occultism. 3. Alchemy. I. Title.
BF1442.M34 M34 200
291.3'7—dc20
2002073254

Contents

INTRODUCTION

"Mandalas? Oh! those weird brightly colored Buddhist diagrams!"

Mandalas have become familiar to people in the West in recent decades through the interest in and publication of Eastern spiritual and esoteric material. The term *mandala* comes from a Sanskrit word meaning 'circle,' and thus is applied to spiritual or metaphysical diagrams arranged in the form of a circle.

Those who have studied Western esotericism in depth will be aware of the fact that 'mandalas' also exist at the heart of Western esotericism, particularly in the Hermetic current. These Western mandalas are, however, much more obscure and have consequently been neglected. They do not have attached to them the aura of the 'mystic East' that Western people in recent times often see in a romantic way as the only true source of spiritual insight. However, they bear within themselves a profound system of spiritual wisdom paralleling that which is found in the Eastern traditions. This book is intended to bring this Western mandala tradition to the attention of the reader, and to provide illustrations and full commentary on a number of examples of such mandalas. The analyses of the mandalas presented here will, we hope, help people gain access to the complex symbolism worked into the Western mandalas. Much of this symbolic material is derived from alchemy, Kabbalah, and Hermetic memory systems, which at first may be rather opaque and obscure to the reader, but I hope that the commentaries will help to make the symbolism more clear and reveal the inner forms of each of these mandalas.

Most of the plates reproduced here are from 16th, 17th and 18th century emblem books, alchemical manuscripts, and from the illustrations to Rosicrucian writings. There is a wealth of such material as yet unexplored which needs to be brought to light, as such emblematic figures contain in an highly compressed and coded form the essence of the Western esoteric tradition. We will find that the symbols woven therein still speak directly to our souls today, and I hope that the sensitive reader will be inspired and encouraged by this book to work further with these mandalas and find the spiritual gold that can be won through contemplating and meditating on these emblems.

Although it would be a useful and valuable exercise to follow up the parallels that undoubtedly exist between the Eastern mandalas and mandalas as they appear in our Western tradition, I do not have the background in the Eastern traditions required to attempt this, and this present book will focus almost entirely on the Western systems. It would be of the greatest delight to me if some other writer grounded in both traditions might be able to contribute a volume on the parallels that exist, as this would provide another layer for our understanding of these enigmatic and mysterious structures of symbols.

In recent times it has been primarily through the work of the psychologist Carl G. Jung (1875-1961) that the symbolism of the Western mandalas has been made approachable. Jung observed a link between the symbolic material arising spontaneously in the dreams of people going through inner crises, and the strange symbols found in alchemical writings and emblems. He came to realize that the psyche is structured around certain 'archetypes' or constellations of symbols, that the tap roots of these archetypes reach deep down into the collective unconscious of mankind, and were laid down in the psyche far back in time. Thus Jung saw the alchemical tradition of the 13th to 18th centuries as a kind of ancient psychic monument and, like an archaeologist, began to dig into this mound of symbolic material, down through past layers in the psyche, in order to find some new insights into and understandings of that which works in our souls today. To Jung there was no contradiction in trying to explain the source and energetics of the struggles of the twentieth century psyche as lying bound up in the 'prima materia,' the symbols of medieval and Renaissance alchemy.

These alchemists were pioneers in a sense, people open to their inner worlds, who 'projected' their inner perceptions onto outer symbols, and thus found a universal language transcending words to communicate their experiences of the soul's architecture. Thus, if we but reverse the process, taking the symbols of these alchemical mandalas and breathing them into our souls, integrating them, weaving them into our innermost being, then we will be able to recapitulate the alchemists' perceptions, touch upon and repeat their profound inner experiences. Thus these mandalas, far from being the amusing and pretty remnants of an ancient medieval tradition, can be seen as keys which unlock the mysteries of the soul's architecture. If we choose to use them in this way, they can lead us deep into the mysteries of our inner world.

The Mandalas as a Neglected Art Form

These Western mandalas are also neglected as sources of inspiration to artists and writers. It has long been known that many artists have been connected with esoteric groups, or in some way have drawn, even if tangentially, upon esoteric ideas. Artists must be open to the impulses of their souls and their sources of inspiration, so it should not be too surprising that some amongst them go further

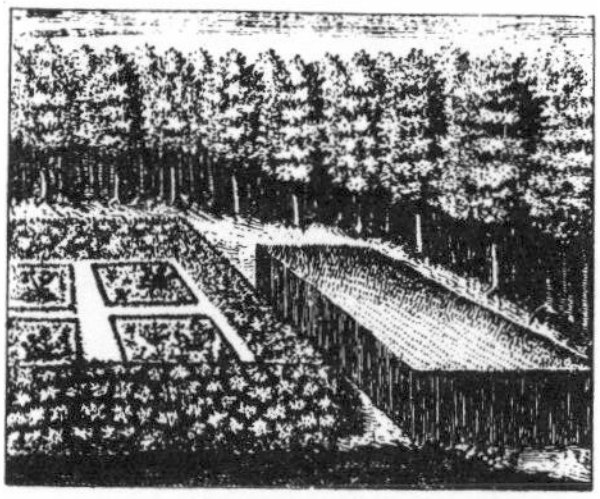

and investigate the traditions and bodies of ideas about the soul and spiritual concerns. Thus some artists have worked within the stream of esoteric ideas which underlies the Western mandalas; for example, we have to recognize the work of Hieronymus Bosch and Jan Van Eyck (creator of the Ghent Altarpiece, and especially the 'Adoration of the Lamb' panel) as elaborate mandalas. We can trace this tradition further through Michelangelo's Sistine Chapel ceiling, on through William Blake's paintings and etchings, right into the Surrealist art of our present century, where again the esoteric ideas underlying such mandalas surface in an artistic movement. We can go further back and find mandalas enshrined in sacred architecture, and especially in the rose windows of the gothic cathedrals, where the art of the mandala is elevated to a profound and moving interweaving of color and form. Even the ancient stone circles and henges may be seen as large scale mandalas worked out on the surface of the Earth by our distant ancestors.

There are, I would suggest, aspects of Western art that remain opaque until one looks at these works with an awareness of the ideas working in the esoteric traditions that were woven into these mandalas. The profound influence of esoteric symbolism on such artworks has not been adequately recognized, and, indeed, the art of the Western mandala is almost entirely neglected. The inspired sense of design, economy of line, and skill of workmanship that went into the early 17th century engravings of the Oppenheim-Frankfurt School of engravers and printers, such as Theodore de Bry, Matthieu Merian and others, is rarely commented upon by art historians; indeed, the alchemical, Hermetic or magical mandalas have yet to be recognized as important influences in the history of Western art. So, even if we lay aside the esoteric implications in and of itself, it is my view that these

Western mandalas are an important though neglected aspect of art history requiring, and indeed crying out for, the attention of scholars and historians of Western art.

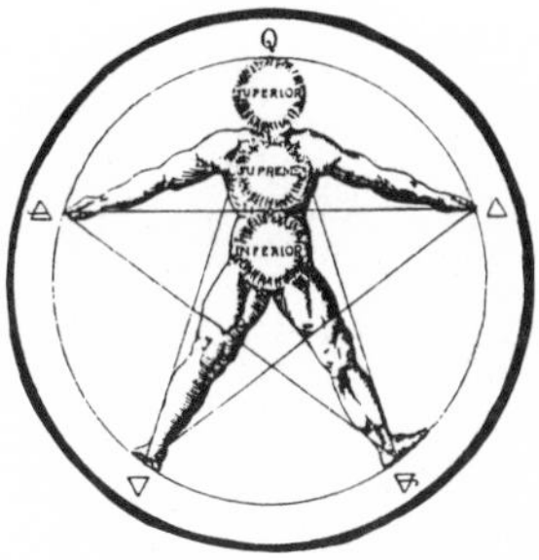

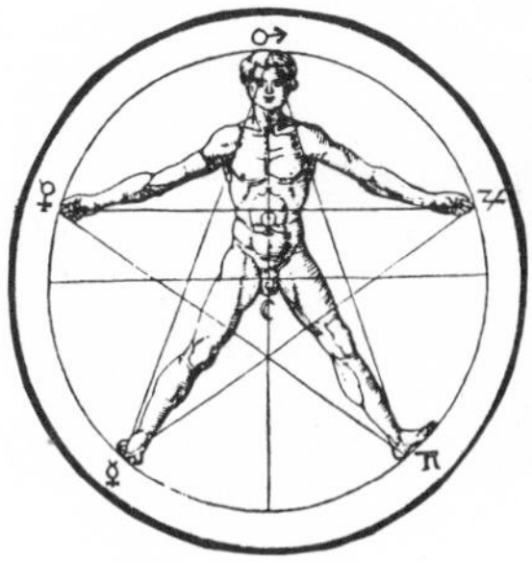

The Symbolic Content of Mandalas

The philosophic and esoteric ideas underlying these mandalas derive from the Hermetic tradition. It would require a lengthy book indeed to adequately document these ideas, but many of them are to a great extent explained in the commentaries to each plate. These commentaries have been arranged to build up sequentially a picture of the ideas working behind the Western mandalas. We find there, for example, an intricate NUMERICAL SYMBOLISM, which is often simultaneously expressed in GEOMETRICAL FORMS:

UNITY: the totality and sum of all, the point at the center of the mandala around which all the symbols are constellated;

DUALITY: the polarities of male and female, heaven and earth, conscious and unconscious, both horizontal polarities and vertical ones;

TRIPLICITY: the Three Principles, Salt, Sulphur, Mercury; the Trinity and its varied manifestations, the third point of the triangle as the resolution of the polarities;

the QUATERNITY of the Four Elements; the solidity of the square; the four archetypal beasts, Lion, Bull, Eagle, and Man;

the FIVEFOLD, the four elements which together with the quintessence form the pentagram;

the SIXFOLD, the six-pointed star, the Seal of Solomon, the intertwined upward and downward pointing triangles;

the SEVEN planets;

the EIGHTFOLD, double quaternary;

the Nine hierarchies of Angels;
the Ten Sephiroth;
the Twelve zodiacal signs.

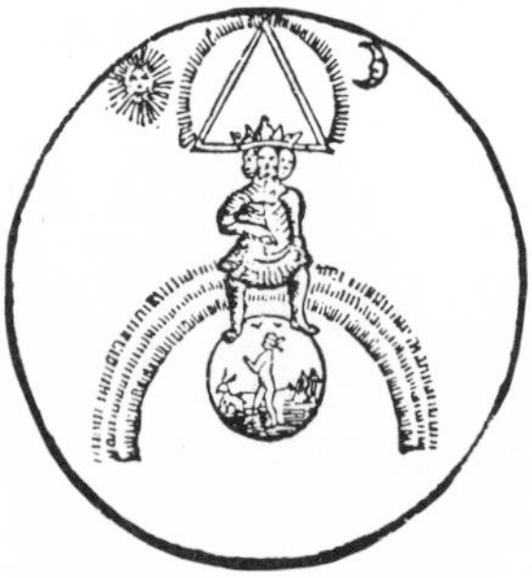

There is a further layer of Animal Symbols, lions, bulls, dragons and serpents, and Bird Symbols familiar in alchemy as phoenix, black crow, peacock with resplendent tail, pelican, white swan and dove, which have precise meanings. There are other Plant Symbols: root, leaf, flower and seed, each having definite meanings, while the tree is often used as an archetypal form for a mandala. Symbolic Objects such as vessels, cups and chalices, and the enclosed spaces of flasks and retorts, will be recognized as having different significances, while distillation apparatus, flasks and receivers, sometimes add a further facet to the operations within vessels. Other objects with special meanings are orbs and scepters, crowns, swords, altars, fountains, and mountains. There also appear Human Symbolic Figures. The King and Queen archetypes often appear, though they can have different meanings within the context of various mandalas. The Old Man is an important symbol often linked with a rebirth as a Young Prince or Knight. The human skeleton also appears as a symbol of the *nigredo* which precedes and is essential to rebirth and transformation.

This symbolic material also appears in the Hermetic tradition in the form of the alchemical allegories. These are elaborate stories in which the central figure is led through a transformative process pictured as a journey, upon which he meets and interacts with the symbols familiar to us in the mandalas: lions, snakes, mountains, castles, kings and queens, crownings and immersions in fountains, deaths and metamorphoses. Allegorical tales such as *The Dream of Poliphilo*, *The Chymical Wedding of Christian Rosenkreutz*, the *Parable* of Hinricus Madathanus, and the fountain allegory of Bernard of Treviso, are another way of working with this symbolic material, perhaps in a more four-dimensional manner, because they involve the passage of time and can therefore reflect transformation in a different way than the mandalas, which are more static in time. I intend to publish a companion volume in this series on these alchemical allegories which, like the mandalas, are equally neglected.

This symbolic material is elaborate and profound and lies at the foundation of the Western psyche. It should not be surprising that working with such symbols can be initially disturbing and disquieting, though one comes eventually through this to an awareness of the transformative power within these symbols. It will be found best not to work with these symbols in isolation, but to experience them within the mandala structure. The Hermetic initiates who wove these figures carefully crafted each mandala to balance the energies of the individual symbols. Thus they incarnated a way of working with these powerful, polarized archetypes that resolves and synthesizes their energies. Within the mandala the energies of these symbols are quite safely balanced, and the beautiful sense of an integrated resolution of symbolic power should warn us against taking the mandalas apart and working with the symbolic fragments, or attempting to create our own mandalas, until we fully understand the forces that work within their forms. We should respect the inner beauty and wholeness of the symbolic architecture of the mandalas.

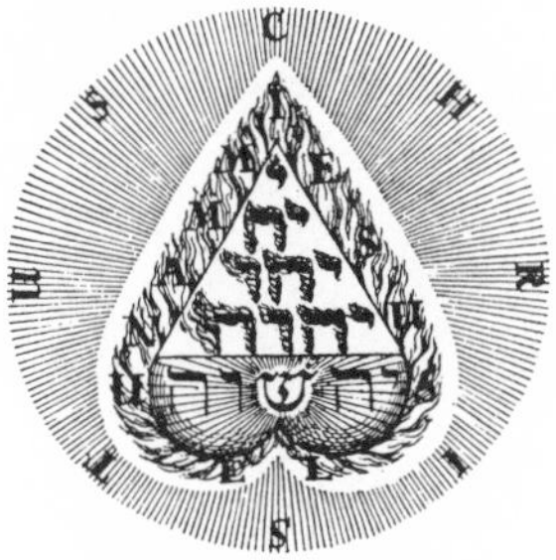

I have been very careful, while analyzing each symbol, to set it against the other symbols with which it is constellated, thus keeping a sense of the synthesis of the symbol within the total space of the mandala. The commentaries are thus not merely intellectual analyses, but essays in the analysis and synthesis of the symbols, the 'solve et coagula,' 'separatio et coniunctio,' the dissolving and coagula-

FLEGMAT
SANGVIN
MELANC
COLERIC

tion, the separation and re-joining together, used as an exercise by the medieval alchemists. These commentaries will be found to form a basis for working with the mandalas inwardly.

In general, mandalas are circular in form with a definite central point around which the symbolism is constellated, and there is a sense of dynamic tension between center and circumference. The center should be, in a sense, empty: a receptive space into which our consciousness can flow and resolve the tensions and polarities inherent in the symbols arranged around this point. Circularity is not mandatory, however, and many mandalas have a four-square form. In the Western traditions, through the influence of Hermetic memory systems, other archetypal mandala forms have been devised. These include TREES, in which the various symbols are arranged on a tree-form with roots, trunk, branches and leaves; TEMPLES, in which the symbolism is arranged as architectural features of a building; or HOLY MOUNTAINS, in which the symbols are placed on a path leading spirally around a mountain of initiation to its summit. This group of mandalas is polarized vertically, as they have a definite bottom and top, and a path of transformation leading from an initial state of being to a goal. Though they are not circular, they work in a similar way to mandalas, and it is my view that they should be included under this term. Some portray a transformation of the lower into the higher, while others in this category reflect a mutual meeting and interrelationship of the above and the below, in a spiritualization of earthly substance and an earthing of the diffuse spirit.

Working with the Mandalas Inwardly

As I have indicated earlier, these mandalas can be seen as keys to an understanding of the psyche. In fact, we should recognize them as threefold—as KEYS, as DOORWAYS, and as PATHWAYS into our inner spiritual realm. Moreover, working with the mandalas should be undertaken on three levels.

Mons
Magorum
Invisibilis
Lumen
Naturæ
Thesaurus Incantatus
Non nisi Parvulis

Jung recognized the psychic component of the symbolic material in these mandalas, and he applied his insights to the realm of the psyche, in the sphere of psychotherapy, for the healing of the soul. Though his work has deeper social, philosophical, historical, and spiritual dimensions, he was not able to pursue all of these facets to their limits. I would like here to indicate some practical ways of working with the mandalas in meditation as a means of inner spiritual transformation.

A First Level of Working: Spiritualizing the Thinking

We have to begin by contemplating the particular mandala we have chosen, looking at it carefully and trying to understand with our intellect all the symbols, numbers and geometric forms that underlie the chosen figure. The reader should carefully study the commentary and try to find further ramifications that I may have neglected or not found space to explore in detail. Mere passive understanding will not lead one very far, but each act of creative thinking over a mandala, each new discovery and original insight, will open up the inner reflections of the symbols, like the turning of a key. Thus I have written the commentaries so that they are not exhaustive, but instead throw out feelers toward other symbolic systems; indeed, I have often suggested avenues for further exploration. It is useful at this stage to work with the mandalas artistically, if one has the ability. For example, one might draw the mandala out in a different style, or perhaps color in the symbols on the mandala in a way that is esoterically suitable, such as by reflecting the elemental or

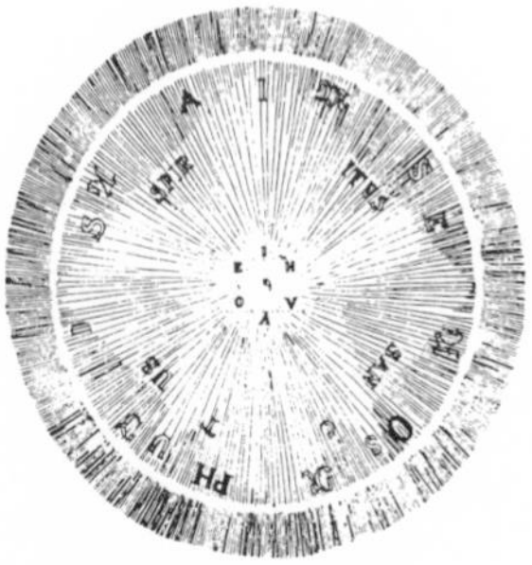

planetary colors, and using complementary colors for the two symbols of a polarity. I have found it of the greatest value to live constantly with these emblems in my environment, on the walls of my study, kitchen or bedroom. Every so often one is rewarded with some new insight.

This first stage will be found to be an experience of the mandala as a KEY to unlocking the symbols within one's being. Through deep study of these mandalas, one's thinking becomes more spiritualized and open to working with symbolic material. Seen esoterically this stage involves the weaving of the symbolic substance of the mandala into our etheric body through the creative use of thought. Some people will stop at this stage and find it valuable in itself to possess this inner key; however, others will want to go further and use the mandalas in meditation. Here they will be found to be GATES or DOORWAYS into the spiritualization of one's feelings.

Meditative Working with Mandalas

This stage can only begin if and when you have worked through the first level and possess the mandala as an inner key woven into the etheric fabric of your being. If you have not done the necessary intellectual work, your meditation may be pretty and delightful, but will have little power to tinge and transmute the flowing energies of your soul. To meditate on a mandala one must know it completely and have a sense of its structure, polarities and symbolic content. Such meditation should not be undertaken when we are too tired—it is a common though understandable mistake for beginners to meditate in the late evening or when in bed before sleeping. There will be no need for special positions or postures. Such meditations involve making an intimate relationship with the soul and are not an experience of energy patterns in the physical or etheric bodies (as is the case with yoga asanas or certain Western magical exercises), so posture is not important except that one is comfortable. Each person will find his own way of balancing his energies: some prefer to sit upright in a chair, others to assume an Eastern 'lotus' or cross-legged position, while others find that reclining in an arm chair or lying flat on the floor or a bed is best. The important thing is comfort and being able to remain quiet in one position for some time without cramps, muscle tension or other discomforts intruding into one's inner work.

Having experimented and found a suitable position, and somewhere where you will not be disturbed for an hour or so, you can begin each session with a short exercise that takes you into your inner space. This is the exercise of the INNER EGG OR RETORT.

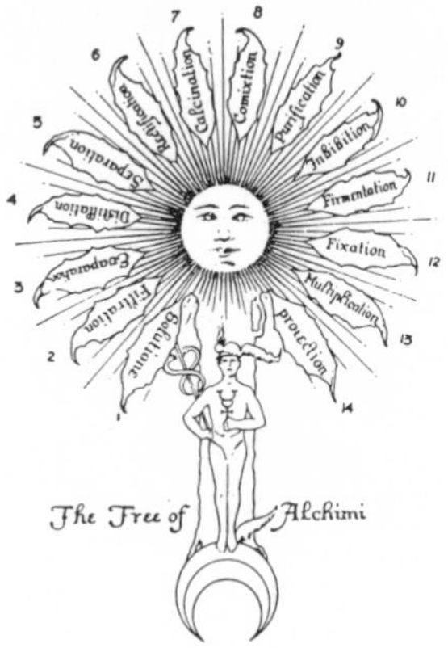
Calcination
Comixtion
Purification
Fermentation
Fixation
Separation
Distillation
Evaporation
Filtration
The Tree of Alchimi

The Inner Egg Meditation

As you begin to settle yourself for this exercise, explore the ways in which your inner being connects with the outer world. Follow out in consciousness, say, your hearing of a slight sound; feel your consciousness raying out to the source of the sound and then returning inwards. Allow yourself to become aware of your bodily posture, of a small discomfort perhaps, and feel through your sense of touch how you connect with the physical world; then allow your consciousness to withdraw and follow this sensation back inward. Continue this with all the senses, using the impulses that come to you through the sense organs in a natural way. Do not try to force or repress these realities, but follow these outward and allow yourself to return inward. You will begin to feel a growing awareness of the relationship between your inner being and your perception, and when this arises naturally in the meditation, begin to inwardly form a picture of this awareness as an Egg or Flask-Retort.

Picture your being as a flask. The outside world can only enter through the walls of this flask, the shell of the egg. Let your consciousness look outward through the walls of the flask into the sense world, and be able to return inward to your soul egg.

As this meditation continues, you will find sudden images, jumbled thoughts, and daily worries arising quite naturally. In this exercise, do not try to repress these or avert your consciousness from them, but allow each of them in turn to develop, grow to fruition, and then dissolve as their energy dissipates. These images and emotional impulses arise out of our unconscious mind, the raw energy of our inner life, the ground of our being. Picture this in the meditation as the most inward content of the flask or egg, a deep interior darkness out of which these impulses unconsciously stir. Allow your being to sink inward, to immerse itself in the inner contents of the flask, and then return to the surface.

You must now begin to bring the parts of this exercise together, picturing your being as the egg or retort, a dynamic boundary between the multiplicity of outer perception and inward streaming unconscious activity. In this meditative exercise, your soul touches upon the two seas in which your being has no firm foundation, and through this inner touching begins to contact the solid ground of the soul which lies between these two realms. Thus you begin to grow a space within, a space in which you can work surely with the soul.

A Second Level of Working: Mandalas as Inner Doorways

You should begin by practicing the Inner Egg meditation by itself, and once you become familiar with it, use it as an opening and closing meditation for your inner work with the mandalas. Each time you meditate put yourself into this secure inner space, then begin to build up in pictures the form of the mandala you have chosen to work with. Visualize the mandala as a panel or door placed before you. As your consciousness shifts and loses the image, try to hold to some fundamental structure in the mandala upon which to rebuild the symbols. You will have to work very hard at first to sustain the inward picture. In time, with practice, this will become somewhat easier as you strengthen the inner symbolic picture building facet of your consciousness. Indeed, the initial difficulties are welcome in that they indicate a learning process has been undertaken inwardly. However, you should not overstrain your consciousness by trying to sustain the mandala inwardly for too long a period. Initially a few minutes is sufficient, and if eventually you can hold the mandala inwardly without it dissolving away or defocusing too often within a five minute period, then you have achieved success. You will find at this stage that the symbols often shift spontaneously, even reversing themselves. You have to enter into this experience consciously.

Once you can inwardly build and sustain the mandala, then you should try to experience your feelings evoked by the symbols. For example, the foursquareness of some mandalas will be found to have a secure and safe feeling. Hold this aspect of the mandala in sharp focus in your meditation and allow yourself to feel the security of the symbol. The symbols of the four elements evoke definite feelings. Try, through exploring the feelings evoked in yourself, to clothe the stark, cold, abstract quality of some of the symbols. Remain outside the symbols of the mandala and do not allow your feelings at this stage to draw you into or merge with the symbols, but keep the mandala before you as a wall panel or decorated doorway. Feel the pride of the lion element, the earthy solidity of the bull, the airy freedom of the bird to soar within the space of the

SPIRITVS SANCTVS
DEVS
PATER
FILIVS
NON EST
SANCTVS
NON EST
SANCTVS
EST
EST
EST

IGNIS
AER
TERRA
AQVA
ACTIVA
PASSIVA
QVINTA ESSENTIA

mandala, the sacrificial gesture of the pelican.

The more you are able to clothe the symbols with your feelings, the more you gain from this exercise. If the feelings prove in any way disturbing or overwhelming, dissolve the mandala and go back to the security of your Inner Egg, and either gently return to outer consciousness or pause for a moment; if you wish, rebuild the inner mandala and try to encounter these feelings again. If you keep the symbols in balance, as I indicated earlier, the feelings evoked will be harmonious. After working with a mandala in this way a number of times, you should have an inner feeling picture, as well as an inner symbolic map, of the mandala. In time, this inner feeling picture or reflection of the mandala in your emotions (esoterically, in your lower astral substance) will present itself to you like a door or gateway. There will be a doorway or passage into a new consciousness of the energies and structures of your inner world.

This is the second level of working with these alchemical mandalas, and if conscientiously undertaken it results in a spiritualization of the feelings and a weaving of the symbolic pattern of the mandalas into the astral substance of the soul. Some people will find this sufficiently rewarding in itself as an exercise and will not need to proceed further, for they will have attained what they needed from working with the mandalas at this stage in their life—a sense, an awareness, of the structure and dynamics of their psyche.

A Third Level of Working: Mandalas as Inner Journeys

A third level of working with mandalas can only be attained by those who have fully experienced the results of the first two stages, being able at will to call up and sustain a mandala, and being able to fill this with emotional currents, thereby reflecting its form in their feelings so that it appears like a door opening within their inner world.

Sigilum Hermetis
C
H
A
O
S
Hiems
Ver
Autumno
AQVA
Sal philosophorum
Æstas

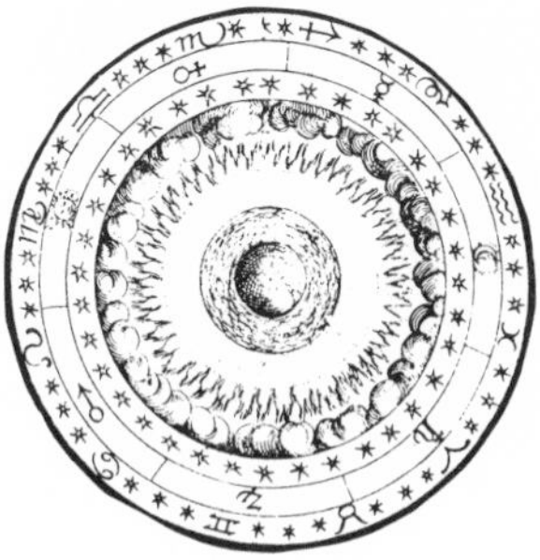

This stage involves constructing the mandala image, not before you as a panel on a vertical wall, but on the ground or floor. A useful opening meditation for this exercise, instead of the Retort or Inner Egg, is to create an inner garden or sacred landscape. This is a space similar to the enclosed inner space of the Egg, but in the form of an enclosed secret or magical garden. (Alternatively, you could use the image of a sacred building or inner temple as an opening exercise form.) In this opening exercise you should picture this garden, say, bounded in the distance by a square or circular high hedge and initially only with a neat flat lawn. You are standing at the center of this garden. It is safe and comforting, a secure base from which to work. You know that you can always return here and rest awhile at any time during the meditation.

Now begin to build the mandala you have chosen on this lawn, and find subtle ways of picturing the symbols. The animals can now be fully three dimensional, either as statues or living beings. Once you have built up this inner garden, sacred enclosure or temple, you must embark upon a journey through the symbols, traveling to each in turn by different routes. The mandala is now to be experienced as surrounding your being, and not placed in front of you or separated from your inner point of soul. You are to will yourself into the space of the mandala, and, on different visits to this inner garden, you can take different paths round the symbols.

The first few times you work with this exercise you will be unable to do anything except sustain the pictures and the layout of your mandala space. However, to begin the true work of this third level of working with the mandalas, you must allow yourself to explore the feelings evoked by meeting with

each symbol on your journey through the mandala. Allow this to go further than the second level: let the symbols, in a sense, take on their own life and not just be reflections of your emotional input. Here you are trying to sense the *being* behind the symbols. This is extremely difficult at first, for, if you allow the symbols any degree of freedom, they can metamorphose alarmingly through a repertoire of forms. You must have patience on your journey and wait for a definite form to emerge. Say a pelican stands at a particular point in the mandala. On a first approach this pelican might appear in a conventional shape. Then, as you inwardly evoke the feeling of the symbol, the element of sacrifice, the pelican might suddenly change into a wound, a crucifixion, an open basin of blood overflowing, a flamingo, a cat suckling her kittens, and so on. As you stand before the pelican, step into the symbol and try to feel the essence of its sacrifice, whether it is guarding a point in the mandala, leading you towards another symbol, or asking you to turn back.

This exercise involves taking an inner journey, and like journeys in the outer world it should be exciting and sometimes disturbing. Some of these symbols can take on seemingly horrific forms, but if you are disturbed by these, merely return to your initial magical garden and decide whether you wish to return to outer consciousness or to re-enter the mandala space and try again to encounter the symbol. Strong, frightening appearances of symbols are as likely to occur as breathtaking, beautifully formed ones, for we are travelling through mandalas with polarities. Each symbol may jump between the poles of attraction and repulsion, between its thesis and antithesis, a fearful form and an enchantingly beautiful one. Contacting these polarities and metamorphoses inwardly in these exercises is a most important step in our spiritual development, as it develops our inner spiritual will to encounter the spiritual being and power working behind these symbols. Us-

ing these mandalas will provide a safe way of working with such symbols, as they are inwardly balanced within the space of the mandala. Any distressing or disturbing energies probably arise because we momentarily lose consciousness of the whole mandala and relate instead to a symbol in isolation. This merely emphasizes the need to work hard at the first two levels before embarking upon the inner journeys of the third level.

These three exercises outlined above are ways of working on different levels to transform our innermost being. The first exercise helps to spiritualize our thinking: it frees our thinking from the purely analytic mode that is bound to the outer material world and which only uses sense perceptions as its *prima materia*. In trying to understand the symbolism within a mandala we will have to use our power of *synthesis* to unite ideas and symbols together, and not merely isolate and examine them analytically and sequentially. Contemplating these mandalas does not primarily sharpen our thinking; rather, it makes our thinking more fluid, enabling it to flow and dance in the mandala space. It etherealizes our thinking, making it less tied to and weighed down by the outer shapes of ideas.

The second exercise results in a spiritualization of our feelings, by allowing our feelings to unfold in our consciousness and reveal themselves in association with archetypal symbols. In fact, these archetypal symbols live unconsciously behind much of our life of feelings as inner shadowy forms or moulds into which our emotional energies pour. Through working with these mandalas, we will become more conscious of these underlying archetypal forms, and gain an understanding of the hidden inner structure behind much of our feeling life. Of course, we will not get results from this overnight, but with perseverance we may find ourselves becoming steadily more conscious of the forces working behind our

ACTIVA
HOMO
PASSIVA

feelings. We become aware of the spiritual energies and patterns lying behind our emotions.

The third stage involves a deeper relationship with the mandala structure. Here we have to step into the inner space of the mandala and be challenged to act within its symbolic framework. Thus our will becomes spiritualized through encountering the elaborate symbolism on the level of action and not just in our thoughts and feelings. In doing these third level exercises, we temporarily live inwardly on the same level as the symbols, sharing the same space with them and experiencing them as archetypes in our will. Those who are able to work through this exercise find their will forces strengthened; they discover a greater degree of personal freedom over the clutter of unconscious promptings and impulses which form the background to much of our life.

We will find that this inner work with the mandalas cannot be confined to periods of meditation. Once we begin to live with these symbols, they will inevitably express themselves through our dreams, creative perceptions, fantasies, and sometimes synchronistically appear in sequences of events, in coincidental happenings in our outer life. If we are to fully enter into the mandala we must be open to these experiences and try to incorporate these perceptions from other levels into our work with the mandalas.

To work successfully with these exercises we should try to see ourselves as alchemists, working upon our inner soul substance, purifying, distilling and transmuting it into a more noble state. Then we will find that these mandalas are not dead fragments illustrating ancient, discredited philosophies, but tools for transforming our souls. When we touch them with our souls through such inner exercises we breathe life into them, begin a dialogue, and set out on a journey through their symbolism—an inner exploration that will tinge, transform and spiritualize our inner life.

These mandalas, like the Philosophers' Stone, carefully crafted by ancient Hermetic initiates of the Western mystery schools, are a precious inheritance and sure foundation upon which we can reintegrate our inner world. They are priceless symbolic tools of transformation, the software or inner programming for unfolding our inner spiritual potential.

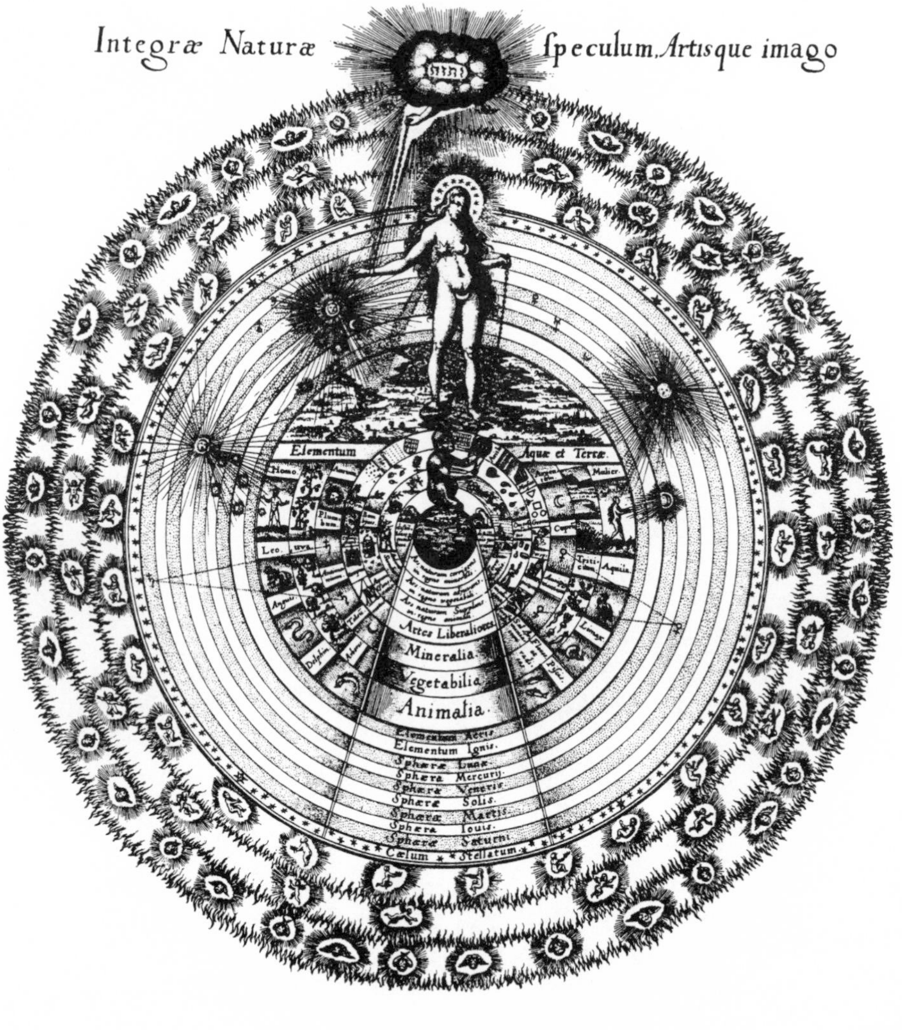
Integræ Naturæ speculum, Artisque imago
Elementum Aquæ et Terræ
Homo
Mulier
Leo
uva
Artes Liberaliores
Mineralia
Vegetabilia
Animalia
Elementum Aeris
Elementum Ignis
Sphæra Lunæ
Sphæra Mercurij
Sphæra Veneris
Sphæra Solis
Sphæra Martis
Sphæra Iouis
Sphæra Saturni
Cælum Stellatum

Illustrations and Commentaries

MANDALA ONE

At the center of all true mandalas is a space into which we can place our consciousness and integrate the symbolism arrayed around this center. The mandala shown opposite is from the *Musaeum Hermeticum*, an early 17th century book, and was used as an aid to meditation on the first seven mystical numbers.

The number one is found in the totality, the wholeness of the symbol which arises out of the alchemist consciously placing himself at the center.

The number two is found in the figures of the King and Queen. The Sun King is mounted upon a lion which stands on a small hillock. He carries a scepter and shield. The Moon Queen is mounted on a whale or dolphin swimming upon the sea. Here we have the male and female archetypes.

The number three appears as the large triangle of Spiritus, Anima, Corpus. The Spirit is connected to the Moon, the Soul with the Solar forces and the Body with the cube of the Earth surrounded by the five other planets, i.e. Saturn, Jupiter, Mars, Venus and Mercury.

The number four forms the corners of the diagram, with, at the top, the salamander of the Fire element, the bird of the Air element, and at the lower corners of the square the Water and Earth elements.

The number five forms the pentangle of the alchemist's body. His right foot is on the earth, his left foot is in the water; his left hand holds a feather symbolizing air, his right a torch or candle of fire, and above his head the two wings indicate the quintessence, the fifth element, or the spirit.

The number six arises out of the outer triangle of the number three in combination with the inner triangle of Sulphur 🜍 , Mercury ☿ , and Salt □ . Salt corresponds to the cube of the earth, Sulphur to the solar forces of the soul, and Mercury to the lunar spirit.

The number seven, the final number in this series, is indicated in three ways in the structure of this mandala:

- by the sevenfold star of the planets
- by the VITRIOL acrostic of seven words: **V**isita **I**nteriora **T**errae **R**ectifando **I**nvenies **O**ccultum **L**apidem, i.e., "visit the interior of the earth, in purifying you discover the hidden stone."
- by the series of seven circles within the angles of the heptagram, which contain a representation of the alchemical process as a cycle from a death stage through a metamorphosis to a final resurrection. (See Mandala Eleven for a detailed explanation of this cycle of symbols.)

As alchemists working through meditation upon this symbol, we begin to

ANIMA
SPIRITVS
CORPVS
Rectificando
Inuenies
Occultum
Lapidem
Visita
Interiora
Terræ

Mandala One.

structure our inner being so that these seven mystical numbers and their interrelationships stand before our soul simultaneously. We therefore create within the ground of our being an independence from a rigid system, an ability to structure our thought and awareness through all systems.

MANDALA TWO

As in all true mandalas, the alchemist stands in the center of this illustration from Barchusen's *Elementa Chemica,* based on the "Crowning of Nature" manuscript. This is the figure with whom we should identify ourselves, integrating the content of the symbols arrayed around him. The flask is the inner world of the alchemist's being, and thus our own being, which, although sealed off hermetically from the outer world, still receives heat from outside.

The alchemist is emerging in consciousness from the water at the bottom of the flask, the **Sea of the Wise**, or the unconscious world within his being, and holds Sun and Moon symbols in his right and left hands respectively. That is, he has achieved a kind of awareness of these archetypal forces in his being, the male/female aspects of his soul—the positive, active, outgoing and passive, receptive states of his being—and through this consciousness he is able to participate in both these elements.

All this takes place in the Flask or Alembic within a threefoldness of Sulphur 🜍 on the left, Mercury ☿ on the right, and Salt ○ above in the neck of the flask completing the triangle. The alchemist must place his dualistic awareness within this triangle, this trinity, of these three principles. **Sulphur** is the expansive, fiery aspect, that which leads from air to fire, from the gross to the subtle; **Salt** is the hardening, contractive tendency, water crystalizing into earth, the subtle becoming gross; and **Mercury** is the most important principle, interweaving between these two extremes. These universal principles are found behind the substances of the outer world, and in the ground of the human soul. (We can connect them with the three gunas of Indian tradition: *rajas, tamas,* and *sattwa*).

This threefoldness is also found in the Flask, in the vertical dimension, with water at the base of the flask and air at the top, while at their interface or junction appears the alchemist.

Also indicated in this mandala is a **bird** flying upwards, representing the spirit of the process. The releasing of spirit from the bounds of the material world is beautifully and aptly expressed in alchemy by the symbolism of the bird as it soars upwards. Once again this corresponds to an inner process in the meditations of the alchemist going through this stage of development, the spiritualization of the personality, and placing his consciousness far above the material realm.

In the neck of the Flask, in the oval symbol for Salt, stands an old man, an example of the 'Wise Old Man' archetype of Jungian psychology, the spiritual guide of the alchemist. Through the bird, the alchemist's inward soaring, he can touch on, communicate and mediate with this higher self. This is his spiritual guide, who stands within the neck, the sealed opening of the Flask, as a guardian of the threshold into the spiritual world.

Seen as a totality, this mandala shows the alchemist, having gone through the *nigredo* or dark night of the soul, standing at the threshold of a kind of inner rebirth. He experiences a dawning of a new awareness, seen in the emergence of the Sun and Moon from the Sea, the unconscious realm within his soul. He does not step into the trap of dualism, as he can integrate his dawning awareness of the Sun and Moon facets of his being within the threefoldness of the principles lying behind the natural world of the elements. He has now developed the bird within his soul, that facet of his inner life which can mediate, within his meditations, with the higher self, the spiritual guide, the guardian of the threshold.

MANDALA TWO.

MANDALA THREE

Within an egg, the inner space of the soul, we find the alchemist in this mandala on the threshold between two realms: that which the alchemist stands upon, and that which is above and surrounding him.

The alchemist is here split **twofold** as a Rebis or 'Two-Thing,' that is, the male and female aspects of the alchemist's being are here experienced as becoming separated, though not independent. This is the stage in alchemy of the Hermaphrodite—Hermes, the male God figure; Aphrodite, the Goddess—in which the alchemist becomes conscious of the male and female aspects of his or her being. These facets do not separate completely, being rather in a state approaching integration, for the two heads are male and female, yet grow out of one body. The male side, on the alchemist's right, holds the compass; the female side, on the left, holds the set-square: two instruments for measuring the Earth, for constructing circles and squares.

The figure stands between two realms:

Above, the seven planets in the spiritual world beam down their influences, indicated by the lines connecting the planetary stars to the body of the hermaphrodite. The Sun on the male side, and Moon on the female side dominate these spiritual archetypes, while Mercury above stands at the point of balance between the facets of male and female.

Below, the alchemist stands on a fire breathing winged dragon who, in turn, stands upon a winged globe, which bears within a square of the Four and a triangle of the Three. The earth globe symbolizes, in this mandala, the raising of the earthly realm towards the spirit: hence it contains the three principles of the etheric realm and the four elements that constitute the physical body. Thus the alchemist through working upon his or her physical and etheric bodies has raised them, ennobled them, out of immersion in the purely physical forces, and has thereby developed a vehicle for higher stages of the Great Work. The dragon is a picture of the lower astral passions, the untamed, unintegrated emotions which pour through the soul. Here the alchemist, in standing upon the dragon, has achieved a degree of mastery, of conscious control. The alchemist, we note, has not destroyed the dragon, for that would cut him off from the raw energy, the fire of the process, but stands above that realm, no longer the dragon's victim, but its master.

Seen as a whole, this mandala pictures the soul of the alchemist at a certain stage of development, when the alchemist—through achieving a degree of purification of the lower vehicles, and a mastery of the lower astral realm—has been enabled to stand upright and receive the influences of the higher nature

REBIS
43

MANDALA THREE.

from the spiritual realm of the planets. At this point in the alchemist's development, he or she becomes aware of the two inward states of soul being that constellate around the male/female polarities, active/passive, analysis/synthesis, etc., which must become integrated consciously as the next stage of the Great Work.

MANDALA FOUR

This illustration, found in the important alchemical text the *Rosarium Philosophorum*, shows us a mandala of the end of the alchemical process which synthesizes the various stages of the Great Work.

The form of the mandala is the integration of the four symbols by the hermaphrodite at the center.

This hermaphrodite is the being of the alchemist, open to an experience of the polarities of male and female, which play through the alchemist's soul. However, a great degree of integration of these two aspects has been achieved, and the twofoldness is now only experienced in the head element of the alchemist. The figure is **winged**, indicating the spiritual nature of the process. The figure is also **crowned**, indicating the attainment of conscious mastery or rulership over the twofoldness. This accomplishment is manifested in the body to the extent that the alchemist is able to balance upon the two horns of the crescent Moon resting upon the Earth.

The golden crown shows rulership of the conscious solar element; the hermaphrodite's balance on the crescent moon shows mastery of the unconscious lunar element. This figure seems almost to float, poised between Heaven and Earth.

At the alchemist's left foot stands the Black Crow or Raven. In one sense this indicates the stage in the alchemical process of inward absorption, of withdrawal from the world of the senses into the inner darkness, the 'dying to the senses.'

At the right foot a tree grows with thirteen moon leaves upon it. One could associate this with the thirteen lunar months in the year, but perhaps esoterically the symbol goes deeper and is a picture of the One and the Twelve. The tree is always a symbol of the connection between the worlds, the growth from one realm into another. 'The One who stands within the Twelve' is a representation of the process of initiation into higher awareness, through integrating these twelve archetypes. This numerical symbolism is found in many mystery traditions.

The alchemist figure holds in his right hand a cup or chalice containing three snakes—the three principles which in outer nature are called Sulphur, Mercury, and Salt, or in the human sphere, Spirit, Soul, and Body. These must be dissolved, merged together in the cup of our being and united, just as in physical alchemy the three principles must be fused together in the crucible.

The hermaphrodite's left hand grasps the Ouroboros, a symbol of the soul taking hold of itself, turning in upon its being and nourishing its own inner life.

We can see the two symbols connected with the female side of the alchemist, the Black Crow stage and the Ouroboros, as being more passive and receptive aspects of inner development, while the Initiation Tree and the Cup of the Three Serpents are more active male facets of the process.

The whole mandala can also be seen as an alchemical version of the pentagram ritual of Hermetic magic, where each point of the pentagram symbolizes an elemental state. The Black Crow, the first point of the invoking ritual pentagram, symbolizes Earth; the Cup symbolizes water, the second point; the Ouroboros, with its soul aspect, is related to the third point of Air; the growth-principle of the Philosophic Tree is related to the fourth point of Fire; and the Crown resting upon the head of the alchemist-hermaphrodite relates to the fifth point, the quintessential element of Spirit.

Mandala Four.

MANDALA FIVE

This well-known plate was originally engraved by Matthieu Merian for Daniel Mylius' *Opus Medico-Chymicum* (1618), but was later included in the *Musaeum Hermeticum* (1678 edition).

In this remarkable mandala of the alchemical process we find the alchemist at the center foreground, standing upon a two-bodied, one-headed lion which disgorges a liquid stream. The alchemist wears a coat of stars—one side (his right) light, the other (his left) dark. He holds in each hand a cleaver, again bearing stars. The alchemist is seen upon a hill with a grove of trees, representing the substance of the physical work: the seven trees of the planetary metals stand on the periphery while, closer to the alchemist, are pictured twelve fundamental substances of the Great Work:

⊖ Salt (♐)	🜍 Sulphur (♈)	♁ Crocus Mars (♌)	Fire
🜿 Tartar (♑)	○ Alum (♉)	✳ Sal Ammoniac (♍)	Earth
⊂⊃ Auripigment (♋)	◷ Vitriol (♏)	⏀ Saltpeter (♓)	Water
⊕ Verdigris (♎)	⸿ Cinnabar (♊)	☿ Mercury (♒)	Air

I suggest the above reconstruction of the elemental correspondences of these symbols based upon another important mandala in Steffan Michelspacher's *Cabala, Spiegel der Kunst und Natur*, 1616, (Mandala Six), where these symbols are related to the twelve signs of the zodiac and thus to the elements.

At the base of the hill, on the alchemist's right, a fire erupts, while on his left a spring of water is seen. On the alchemist's right a male figure is seen, under a light sky, whose left hand is chained to the spiritual realm above. This figure supports a Sun with his right hand, and he is aided in this task by a Lion rampant. These two stand upon stars and the wings of a Phoenix, which has dominion over the spheres of air and fire. On the alchemist's left, a female figure is seen under a dark sky. Her right hand, which holds a bunch of grapes, is chained to the spiritual realms above. This figure supports a Moon with her left hand, and is helped in her task by a Stag of twelve star points. These two stand upon an Eagle, who has dominion over the spheres of water and earth.

Thus we find here a picture of the alchemist integrating the dark unconscious side of his being with the conscious light side, these two being related to the polarities of Male/Female, Right/Left, Fire-Air/Water-Earth, Phoenix/Eagle, Sun/Moon. That he has achieved to a great degree the integration of

VENTORVM-ANNVS SOLARIS-ANNVS STELLATVS-ANNVS
Aquila
Phœnix

MANDALA FIVE.

these facets is indicated by the two-bodied, one-headed lion, the two separate aspects having fused in the head. He also holds the two astral cleavers, which give him the power of discrimination and freedom, yet unlike the two archetypal figures of male and female, who are but puppets of the spiritual world, the alchemist here is truly human, having achieved the independence of his spirit.

Thus we can see what is revealed in the horizontal axis of this mandala. The vertical axis extends these relationships into the three realms of the alchemical process.

Below, on the hill of alchemy, the alchemist stands in the grove of Physical Alchemy, surrounded by the substances of the Great Work.

Above, in the realm of the Soul, the astral world, the middle region, we find the seven spiritual stars and the five birds of Soul Alchemy. These represent inner psychic experiences which the alchemist must go through in the great alchemical work of soul purification. First, the Black Crow or Raven stage, the nigredo, the blackening; second, the White Swan, or albedo, the whitening; third, the Winged Dragon or Cockerel; fourth, the sacrificial element of the Pelican stage; and finally the alchemical resurrection of the Phoenix.

Above, in the brilliant, light-filled realm of the Spirit, we find the nine Hierarchies of Spiritual Beings, and the symbols of the Trinity: the Father יהוה, the Son as the Lamb, and the Holy Spirit represented by the dove.

Between the astral and the spiritual realms a series of circles integrate the symbolism in a threefold way. These stand between the seven planets of the astral realm and the twelve zodiacal signs of the spiritual world. Here we find the triplicities:

Year of the Winds	Year of the Sun	Year of the Stars
Mercury of the Wise	Corporeal Mercury	Common Mercury
Fixed Sulphur	Volatile Sulphur	Combustible Sulphur
Central Salt	Elementary Salt	Earthly Salt

Finally, in the center, we find the statement, "four kinds of fire are required for the work."

MANDALA GROUP SIX

In this special mandala group we will illustrate and describe the four important plates from Steffan Michelspacher's *Cabala, Speigel der Kunst und Nature,* published in Augsburg in 1616, and believed to have distinct Rosicrucian associations. These four plates have never been reproduced and commented upon as a whole, although plate three is well known and has been used as an illustration in many popular books on the occult in recent years. The plates were engraved by Raphael Custodis. Nothing is known of the identity of Michelspacher, though it is usually assumed that this was a pseudonym. The book in which the plates appeared was published in 1616, the same year as *The Chymical Wedding of Christian Rosenkreutz,* and at the height of the Rosicrucian furor.

Plate One:
The Mirror of Art and Nature

Although not a mandala proper, plate one introduces the three mandala plates which describe the alchemical process under the titles 'The Beginning,' 'The Middle' and 'The End.' This introductory plate is divided into three separate bands.

The Upper Section: Here we find two pillars. The one on the left is labeled NATURE and under it stands the alchemist holding in his left hand a book declaring the PRIMA MATERIA, the first matter, or the matter of the beginning of the work; in his right hand he carries the prima materia in a threefold vessel, in which is seen the symbol ♁ . On the right, the alchemist appears again under the pillar labeled ART. Here he carries in his right hand a book declaring the ULTIMA MATERIA, the final substance of the work, which he holds in his left hand. It is contained in a double-interconnected vessel, with the inverse symbol ♀ .

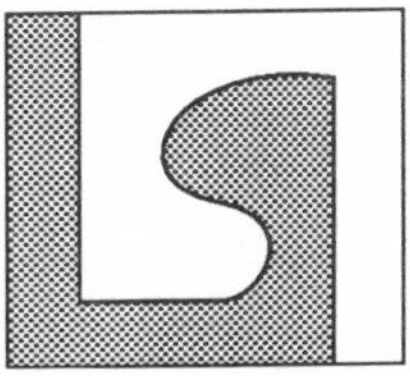

In the center is portrayed the arms of the art of alchemy, with the supporters EAGLE on the left and LION on the right. The shield is divided fourfold, with two quarters bearing three different shaded spheres (the Three Principles), while the other quarters display a symbol which can only be a Western alchemical equivalent of the meeting of Yin and Yang, the primal polarities of the cosmos.

The floor is tiled with square and circle motifs, which indicate that the Great Work involves the squaring of the circle.

The Middle Section: Two panels correspond with the pillars of Nature and Art shown above: on the left is shown the act of mining minerals within the earth that have been brought to a certain state of ripeness by Nature; on the right is depicted the processing above ground through which man by Art completes the ripening of the metals.

In the center are found two circular diagrams with the German Gott (the name of God) around the outside, and also the Alpha and Omega Ⓐ, and the monogram , which may represent the Hebrew name of God, Agla.

The mandala on the left is divided into 360 degrees. Two serpents are entwined around a circle containing a square and a triangle, with letters which respectively form VITRIOL and AZOTH. The circular structure is topped by the symbol introduced above for the Prima Materia , and around the outside of this arrangement are the Four Qualities: heiss = hot, trucken = dry, feucht = moist, and kalt = cold.

The mandala on the right is fourfold, with the Four Elements in the outer circle: fever = fire, erdt = earth, lufft = air, and waser = water. The virtues of Philosophy, Astronomy and Alchemy are indicated in the intermediate ring, and within the central space around the square are shown four substances of the Art: Sulphur, Antimony, Vitriol, and Bismuth (Wismatt). The central octagram has an interesting form. In it the symbol of the Sun is central. In the four innermost vertices of the octagram the Moon symbol is prominent, while in the other set of vertices four Mercury symbols are found. In the eight triangular sections between these points of the octagram, the symbols for the other planets are repeated twice, and are arranged in such a way that Venus is opposite to Mars (solar planets) and Jupiter is opposite to Saturn (lunar planets).

Lower Section: This pictures the alchemist physically at work with substances in the laboratory. A number of different furnaces are shown.

In this plate we have a picture of the three domains of alchemy: the physical work is shown in the lowest section, the soul work with the integration of symbolism through the mandalas is depicted in the middle section, while in the uppermost section the spiritual principles of alchemy are indicated.

Plate Two:
The Beginning: Exaltation

The first true mandala of this series brings together the basic elements that constitute the beginning of the work of alchemy. The word 'CABALA' below is the title of Michelspacher's book. Around the outside, four words proclaim the virtues of Philosophy, Astronomy, and Alchemy.

I. SPIGEL DER KVNST VND NATVR.

NATVR
KVNST
Cabala und die Alchymei,
Geben dir die hochste artzney.
Dar zu auch den weißen Stein,
In dem das fundament allein.
Ligt, wie fur augen zu sehn ist,
In disen figurn zu der frist.
Ach Gott hilf das wir danckbar sei,
Fur diese Gab so hoch und rein.
Der da volkomen ist hierin.
Zu bereitten hie Dises Werck,
Dem sey gegeben alle Sterck.
PRIMA MATERIA
HEISS
TRVCKEN
KALT
FEVCHT
T
R
I
V
L
ZOT
PHILOSOPHIÆ
ERDT
ASTRONOMIÆ
WASER
ALCHIMIÆ
LVFFT
VIRTVTES
FEVER
SVLPHVR
WISMATT
VITRIOL
ANTIMONIVM
Raphael Custodis. sculpsit.
Stephan Michelspacher Ex:

Mandala Six: Plate One.

This mandala consists of an outer circle and a central flask. Around the outer circle are arranged various outer facets of alchemy, the substances, planetary and zodiacal influences, and so on, while within the central flask the inner processes of alchemy are symbolically described.

The Outer Circle is divided into the 360 degrees of the zodiac. The 23 letters of the alphabet are arranged around this circle, and various substances and processes with these initial letters are named:

A Aurum - Gold
B Bley - Lead
C Cheyri
D Dracken Blutt - Dragon's Blood
E Eisen - Iron
F Farb des Werks - (Colors of the Work)
G Grad des △ - Grades of Fire
H Haupt des Rabe - Head of the Crow
I Iovis - Jupiter
K Kopffer - Copper
L Luna - Moon
M Mercurius - Mercury
N Natur - Nature
O Oleum - Oil
P Potabile - Potabile
Q Quinta Esse - Fifth Essence
R Rebis - Hermaphrodite
S Salmiac - Sal Ammoniac
T Tragant - Tragacanth
V Vitriol - Vitriol
X Essig - Vinegar
II Ignis - Fire
Z Zinobar - Cinnabar

The zodiacal circle surrounds a space in which is seen a threefold mandala centered upon a flask. Below this flask stands a strange hybrid beast which bears some of the characteristics of the Four Holy Living Creatures: the Bull's horns, the Man's face, the Lion's body, and the Eagle's talons. Strangely enough, the beast is given a feminine form in that it bears three udders. It wears a triple crown of the three principles, and out of its mouth flows a liquid stream. The beast occupying the space between circumference and center indicates the inharmonious, undigested, integration of the four archetypal creatures—Lion, Bull, Eagle and Man—and the male and female aspects. If the alchemist is to succeed in his task he must create in himself a more harmonious integration. This inner process is sketched in the central flask. The beast stands in a realm in which three globes, containing the zodiacal signs, are arranged at the vertices of the triangle of the Three Principles—Sulphur 🜍 , Mercury ☿ , and Salt 🜔 .

The Central Flask: Within the flask at the center of this mandala an ascending series of animal forms are seen which relate to the stages of alchemy pictured as Alchemical Birds (see Mandala Thirteen). The Lion and Cockerel

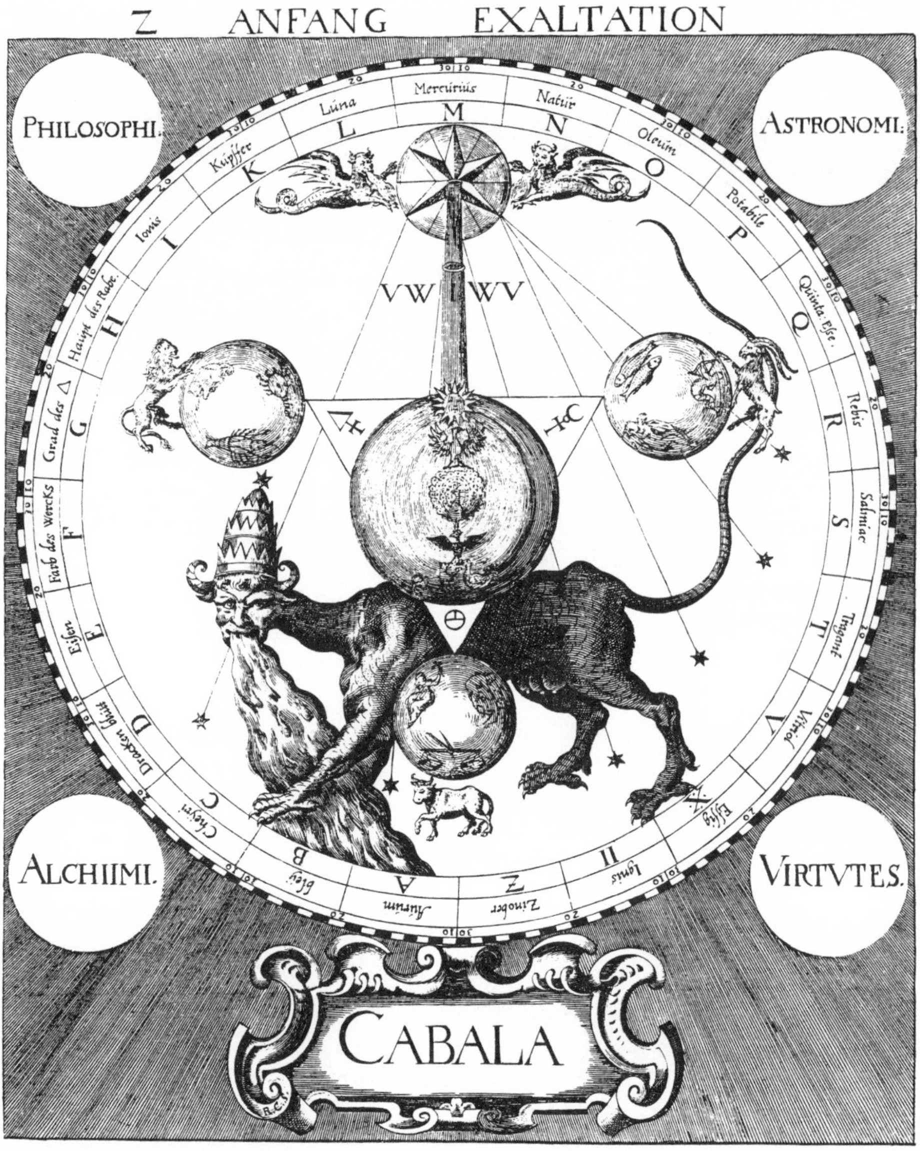
Z ANFANG EXALTATION
PHILOSOPHI.
ASTRONOMI:
ALCHIIMI.
VIRTVTES.
Mercurius
Luna
Natur
Kupffer
Oleum
Ionis
Potabile
Quinta: Esse
Rebis
Salmiac
Farb des Wercks
Eisen
Tragant
Vitriol
Cheyri
Essig
Bley
Ignis
Aurum
Zinober
VW WV
CABALA

Mandala Six: Plate Two.

at the bottom indicate the two primal dualities that constitute the beginning of the process. These come together and lead to the Black Crow stage, then to the stage of the Peacock with its splendid tail, and finally to the stage of the Phoenix, which leads to the solar rebirth as the end of the process. Above, at the neck of the flask, a six-pointed star rays down six stars into the depths of the mandala circle. This star is flanked by two fire breathing dragons, as opposed to the water-breathing beast below.

Plate Three:
The Middle: Conjunction

The most well known of these four plates is a mandala showing the integration of the work in the interior of the earth.

Below, in the foreground, the blindfolded alchemist needs guidance in his quest for wisdom of the workings within the interior of the earth substance. He seeks to grasp its inner essence by ferreting out knowledge of that which lies within, and is depicted in search of this fleeting wisdom by pursuing a rabbit which is burrowing into the earth at the base of the cosmic mountain.

This mountain is surrounded by the zodiac, within the foursquare elements of Fire, Air, Water, and Earth. Each sign of the zodiac is associated with the symbol of a chemical substance. (See Mandala Five.)

♉ Taurus	☿ Mercury	♊ Gemini	🜓 Cinnabar
♎ Libra	🜨 Verdigris	♋ Cancer	🜽 Auripigment
♏ Scorpio	🜖 Vitriol	♐ Sagittarius	🜔 Salt
♈ Aries	🜍 Sulphur	♓ Pisces	🜕 Saltpeter
♌ Leo	🜚 Crocus Mars	♑ Capricorn	🜿 Tartar
♍ Virgo	🜹 Sal Ammoniac	♒ Aquarius	○ Alum

The Mountain is in the form of a pyramid of four steps, with the classical images of the seven planets. On the left side are the **solar planets**: Venus, with flaming heart and looking-glass; Mars, with shield and sword; Sol, with scepter. On the right side, we find the **lunar planets**: Saturn, as Chronos with child and scythe; Jupiter, with scepter and thunderbolt; and Luna, as Diana the huntress with spear and hunting horn. Mercury, as Hermes, holds the summit of the Mountain with winged sandals and helmet, and, holding the caduceus, he stands upon a little fountain contained in a three sided garden.

Within the Mountain lies the Temple of the Sun and Moon, which is approached by an ascent of seven steps, each of which represents an alchemical

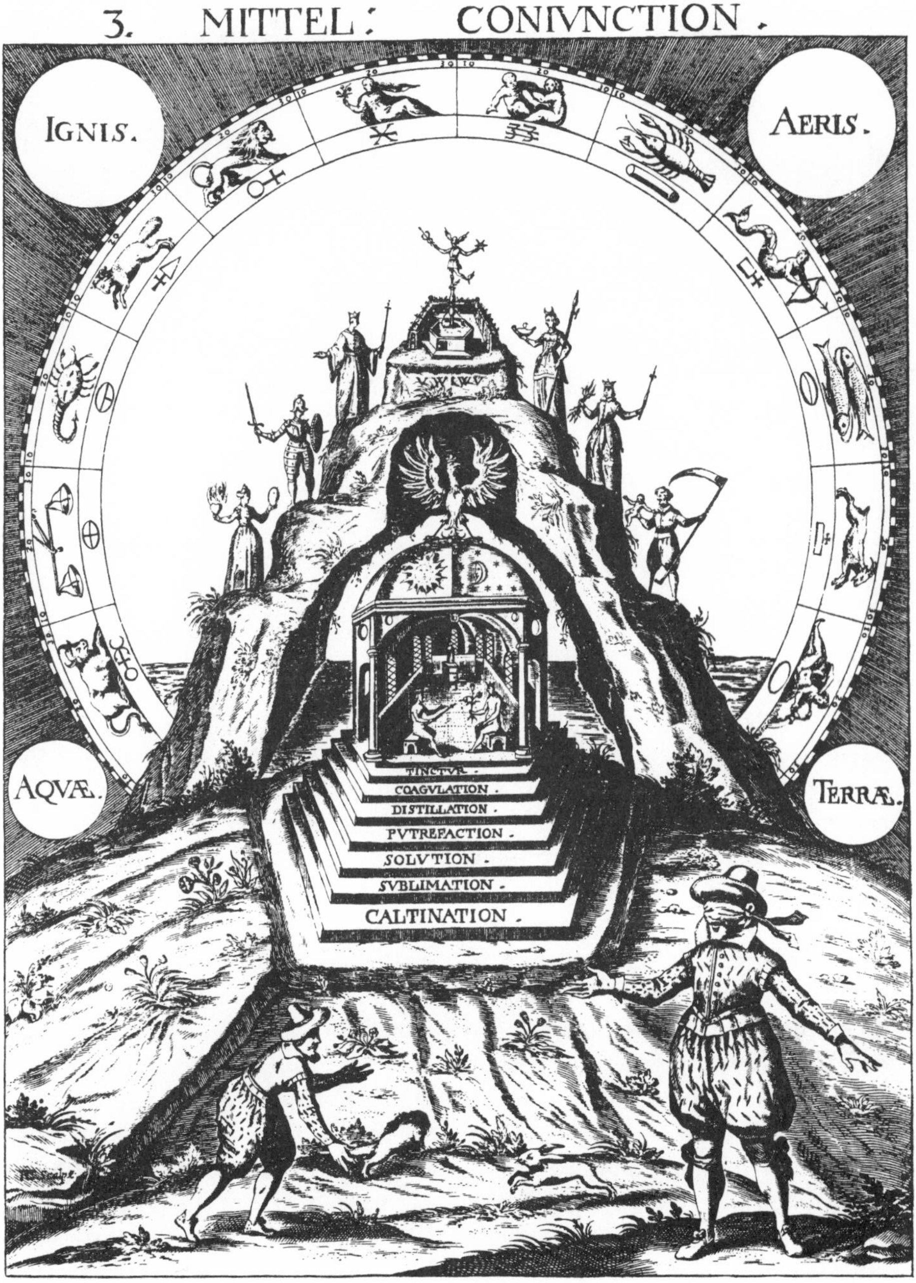
3. MITTEL: CONIVNCTION.
IGNIS.
AERIS.
AQVÆ.
TERRÆ.
TINCTVR.
COAGVLATION.
DISTILLATION.
PVTREFACTION.
SOLVTION.
SVBLIMATION.
CALTINATION.

MANDALA SIX: PLATE THREE.

process: Calcination, Sublimation, Solution, Putrefaction, Distillation, Coagulation and Tincture. These lead one into a vaulted Temple with seven windows in the center of which sits, on the left, the solar King holding a scepter in his right hand, and on the right, the lunar Queen holding a threefold plant in her left hand. Behind them, and completing a triplicity, stands a little alchemical furnace, foursquare at the base and circular at the top. The roof of the Temple carries the symbols of the Sun and Moon, and, as the side of the Moon also has the stars, Day and Night are also implied. Surmounting the Temple roof, a bird in phoenix gesture stands triumphant.

This engraving implies that the alchemist seeking out spiritual wisdom must work with the twelve substances of the Art, and bring them into relationship with the seven planetary forces, within the Earth realm, through a series of seven processes. This will lead him to the Conjunction in the temple under the Earth, the uniting of the King and Queen, Male and Female, Sun and Moon. The achievement of this Conjunction is pictured by the crowned bird in the phoenix gesture.

Plate Four:
The End: Multiplication

At the conclusion of the work, the five alchemists in the dark lower part of the engraving, having reached the summit of their labors by working through the five planetary archetypes ♂ , ♀ , ☿ , ♃ , ♄ , achieve a vision of the two fiery swords which guard the gate of the Garden of Eden. They penetrate through this to a higher vision of the workings of the spiritual world, here pictured within a rainbow. In a foursquare garden there is a vineyard, bowered on three sides. The King and Queen, on left and right, kneel before a FOUNTAIN OF LIGHT, the foundation of which is a six sided basin or bath, upon which sits the Crowned Christ, holding out two chalices, one in each hand, to the kneeling King and Queen. The Fountain is in four tiers. The upper tiers contain respectively the balancing forces of Mars and Venus, Saturn and Jupiter, and the twofold Mercury alone on the upper tier. This fountain is nourished by two sources: At the upper right, an angel turns the screw of a winepress in which Christ with his cross is pictured. From the body of Christ crucified is extracted the essence, which streams down along the Earth to the Fountain of Light, with its enthroned and arisen Christ. From the upper left, where the Divine Name (יהוה) is seen in a nimbus of light, a haloed dove descends to the Fountain with a gift of spiritual power. A triplicity is completed by the dove of the Christ spirit that ascends and returns to the Father from the crucifixion scene.

4. ENDT. MVLTIPLICATION.

V.W.I.W.V.
DER BRVN DES LEBENS.

Mandala Six: Plate Four.

The Series Seen as a Totality

In the first introductory plate there are pictured the three domains of alchemy. This threefold division is amplified and applied to the alchemical process itself by the other three plates.

Plate Two, The Beginning of the Work, draws our attention to the cosmic aspect of alchemy, the working with cosmic substance. In this plate we are far removed from the earthly world. The alchemist, at the beginning of the work, must achieve an exaltation of his vision, and he must glimpse the cosmic significance of the substances and processes with which he is to work.

In the **Third Plate**, The Middle of the Work, the alchemist must unite his exalted perception of the cosmic aspect with the earthly realm. He must seek the spirit in the interior of the Earth, in the very essence, the core, of substance. There he must join together, in a new synthesis, the polarities, the zodiacal archetypes, the planetary forces, the seven processes of alchemy, and the solar and lunar aspects. All of these are found in the Cosmos, the earthly substance, and also in the inner being of Man, the soul of the alchemist himself.

The **final plate** indicates The End of the Work; this is pictured through the image of Christ as the New Adam, the Reborn Adam, Man reunited with his spiritual essence. Christ achieved the true conjunction in that he united the highest spiritual essence with the earthly body of Man, and through this Conjunction, which reached its apotheosis on the Cross, achieved the power of raying out his spiritual forces. This is pictured through the nourishment of the Fountain of Light by the Blood of Christ. In this sense, Christ achieves the Multiplicatio, his blood becoming the tincting Philosopher's Stone, the Stone of the Wise. In this final plate, we see pictured the spiritual connection between the Grail mystery and the mystery of alchemy in the Chalices which Christ holds forth, and in the living spiritual blood that flows from the wound in his side into the Fountain of Light. In this sense, we can identify this series of plates with the spiritual impulse of the Rosicrucians, who sought to bring the ancient wisdom of alchemy into a new living relationship with the inner, esoteric stream of Christianity.

The high spiritual nature of the task before the alchemist is proclaimed in the two verses that stand at the head of the first plate:

Cabala and Alchemy
Give you the highest medicine
As well as the Stone of the Wise
In which alone the foundation rests
As can be seen to this day
In these figures by anyone who has eyes

Oh God, help us to be thankful
For this gift so high and pure
He whose heart and mind you open up
And who is perfect in these
To him will be given all strength
To accomplish this work.

MANDALA SEVEN

This mandala which appears in Daniel Stolcius' *Viridarium Chymicum* of 1624 (*The Chemical Pleasure Garden*) and later in the *Geheime Figuren*, Altona 1785, (*Secret Symbols of the Rosicrucians*), brings together various symbolic elements which we are now familiar with through our studies of the mandalas.

Around the outside we see the seven lettered VITRIOL acrostic (compare with Mandala One)—Visita Interiora Terrae Rectificando Invenies Occultum Lapidem—"visit the interior of the Earth, in purifying you discover the Hidden Stone."

From the border of the space of the mandala two hands reach inward to the center. The left and the right hands indicate the important work the alchemist must undertake in order to unite the primal dualities of his being.

At the lower part of the mandala space two spheres are seen—the Sphere of the Earth Globe, and the Sphere of the Heavens—indicating the need to unite the primal dualities of the Above and the Below, the Cosmic and the Earthly.

In the upper part of the mandala space a cup is seen receiving the forces pouring out from the Sun and the Moon. The other planets are arrayed in such a way as to form the balanced pairs of ♂ Mars and ♀ Venus; and ♄ Saturn and ♃ Jupiter. The more masculine planets are on the left and the more feminine planets are on the right, while the twofold Mercurius ☿ stands below the cup on the exact central line of the mandala space, uniting the polarities within itself.

The central space of the Mandala is occupied by a ring which is linked by a chain into a circular arrangement of three shields. These bear the symbols of the double headed Eagle of the left, the Lion on the right, and the Heptagram below. Thus we have the four symbols of the elements: the Cup of Water, the Eagle of Air, the Lion of Fire, and the Pentacle of Earth. This pentacle is the reflection of the planetary forces in the earth substance. Above the Heptagram shield can be seen the Vitriol symbol ⊖ .

The central space of this mandala is blank and surrounded by a ring to which are chained the elements. Above, the archetypal planetary forces array themselves in a pattern which dynamically balances their inherent duality. These forces, however, meet in Mercury standing just above the center, while below is pictured the symbol of the other primal substance of the work, VITRIOL.

The hidden Stone of the Philosophers arises out of a meeting of Mercury—bearing within it the resolution of the archetypal planetary forces—and Vitriol, the acidic, penetrating essence that leads one into the very of heart of material substances, into the center of the earth.

VISITA INTERIORA TERRÆ RECTIFICANDO INVENIES OCCULTUM LAPIDEM

MANDALA SEVEN.

MANDALA EIGHT

This mandala, George Ripley's Wheel, is normally included in the various editions of his alchemical classic, *The Twelve Gates*, and differs from previous mandalas in this series in that it consists entirely of words without symbols. It thus conveys its meaning directly through the geometrical arrangement of ideas.

This mandala basically synthesizes the fourfold division of the world into one. That is, it leads from a quadrangular perception of the world structure to a circular one. At the center we find the Central Stone uniting the four elements, and around this the first circle proclaims:

When thou hast made the quadrangle round,
Then is all the secret found.

Having recognized the basic structure of this mandala, we note the four outer circles relating to the four elements with their usual correspondences:

FIRE	EARTH	WATER	AIR
hot and dry	cold and dry	cold and moist	hot and moist
Summer	Autumn	Winter	Spring
South	West	North	East

We also find four descriptive qualities which are of great interest:

Attractive	Retentive	Expulsive	Digestive

These four outer circles exist as independent realms, and they become unified by being incorporated into the main body of the mandala through a series of concentric circles. They descend to the inner unity of the Central Stone, described above. In the first ring inward from the four outer elements, we find them incorporated again as four globes fixing the outer dimensions of the Stone. The texts lying within the next inner circle relate to these globes.

The first side of the Stone is in the West, and indicates the entry into the PRACTICE of the Work of the Stone. The text reads

Here the red man to his white wife
Be spoused with the spirit of life

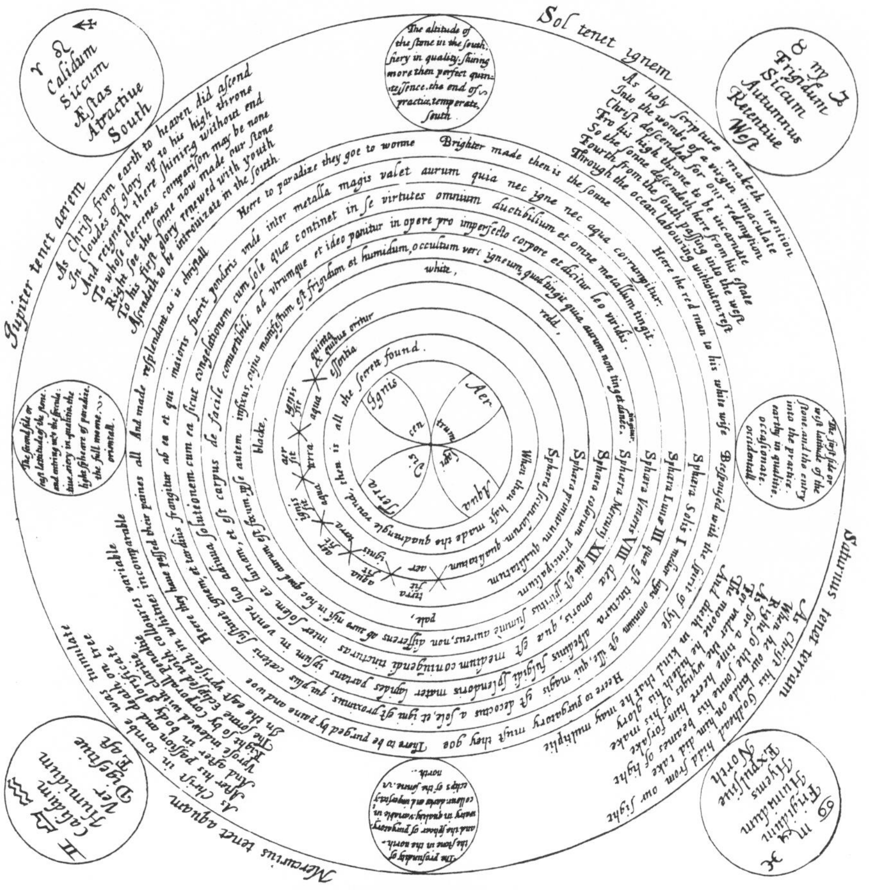

Sol tenet ignem
Jupiter tenet aerem
Saturnus tenet terram
Mercurius tenet aquam
Calidum Siccum Æstas Atractiue South
Frigidum Siccum Autumnus Retentiue West
Frigidum Humidum Hyems Expulsiue North
Calidum Humidum Ver Digestiue East
As holy scripture maketh mention
As Christ from earth to heaven did ascend
Brighter made then is the sonne
Heere to paradize they goe to wonne
Heere the red man to his white wife
Ignis
Aer
Terra
Aqua
centrum
When thou hast made the quadrangle round, then is all the secrett found.

Our heaven this Figure called is
Our table also of the lower Astronomy
Which vnderstood thou may not misse
To make our Medicen parfetly
On it therefore set thy study
And vnto God both night and day
For grace and for yͤ Author pray

} *Cælum Philosophorum*

Mandala Eight.

In the next stage,

Here to purgatory must they go
There to be purged by pain and woe

The globe in the North, the lower dimension of the Stone under which lies the abyss, indicates the role of purification, 'the Sphere of Purgatory,' in the work. (Purification here relates both to the outer substance of the physical work and the inner realm of the soul.)

In the following stage, in the East directly opposite the first globe, we find the entry into the SPECULATIVE part of the work after the purification:

Here they have passed their pains all
And [are] made resplendent as is crystal

The Practice of the Stone encompasses the outer workings which deal directly with substance in experiments. The Speculative ('seeing') aspect of the Stone encompasses the inner experiences that arise in the soul through this outer work.

The uppermost globe, which represents the heights of the Stone, is introduced by the verse

Here to paradise they go to won
Brighter made then is the Sun

This indicates the end of the practice of the Stone, which is thus "shining more than the quintessence."

Between these four stages of the globes, four seven-line verses parallel the alchemical work with the four spiritual transition stages in the life of Christ: the Incarnation, or Descension; the Passion; the Resurrection; and the Ascension.

There follows a series of four spheres, related to the Sun, Moon, Venus and Mercury, which correspond to different facets of the tinctures:

I. THE SPHERE OF THE SUN relates to the best Stone, which is ripened by the Sun, is close in nature to the fire, and sustains the fire of the other stones. Gold, the Sun metal, is the greatest among metals, and neither fire nor water corrupts it.

III. THE LUNAR SPHERE represents the white tincture of flashing splendor, the mother giving birth to these stones in her womb. This tincture promotes solution as the Sun brings congelation, since she contains in herself all the virtues of softening and also tinges all metals.

VIII. THE SPHERE OF VENUS, marked VIII, which stands between the tinctures of the Sun and the Moon, is called the Green Lion.

XII. THE MERCURY SPHERE, XII, in the highest degree the Golden Spirit, does not differ from Gold, except that Gold is fixed, whereas this is unfixed and manifests coldness and moistness, and its fire is hidden.

The next sphere inward indicates the principal colors of the work: Pale, Black, White and Red.

Then we have the sphere of the first and second qualities,

Earth being as Air   Water being as Fire   Air being as Earth   Fire being as Water

from which is born the Fifth Essence (the engraver here seems to have made a slip at this point and repeats the two final terms of the series).

Thus we arrive at the central resolution of this mandala, with its uniting of the fourfold into the one Central Stone.

MANDALA NINE

The mandala opposite has definite Rosicrucian connections in that it appeared in Theophilus Schweighart's *Speculum Sophicum Rhodo-Stauroticum* of 1618, the title page of which indicates that the book was in harmony with "the enlightened Fraternity of the Christian Rose-Cross."

This mandala indicates the threefold nature of Alchemy.

On the summit of a hill stands a tent or tabernacle bearing upon its top the four lettered name of God. Within this tent an alchemist who is "with God" (cum Deo) works the SPIRITUAL ALCHEMY through inner prayer, contemplation of the Divine, and aspiration. This is the higher "work" (ergon).

Below, in two grottos within the hill, the parergon or "subsidiary work" is undertaken. Soul alchemy is portrayed on the left, while physical alchemy is shown on the right.

The work of Soul Alchemy is shown symbolically by the male figure wading through the waters of unconsciousness in his soul, bearing a pot (the vessel of his consciousness) and a spoon with which to fill it. One of the tasks of SOUL ALCHEMY is to inwardly experience and bring into consciousness that which resides in the unconscious sphere. This process involves a soul purification through meditative exercises, symbolized by the bucket in which some clothes are being washed, and by the rain which falls and washes clean. The unconscious element of the soul is, in a sense, the *prima materia* of the work of Soul Alchemy.

On the right, in the domain of PHYSICAL ALCHEMY, the alchemist is portrayed with his furnaces and vessels, and is working to grasp "Nature through the Art." He has achieved a degree of success and clasps the flask, in which the essence of his labors is contained, to his bosom. The four lettered name of God also makes its appearance in this realm following the maxim 'as Above, so Below.' ("T.S.C." is probably **T**heophilus **S**chweighardt **C**onstantiensem.)

These lower realms are cut off within the body of the mountain from the higher Spiritual Alchemy, but they are linked by the winged female Sophia figure supported upon a column stating "This is Wisdom." This figure represents the spiritual potentiality in the soul. Flowing into her being are the energies of the Sun and Moon archetypes which give rise to the gestation of the Soul Child, the slowly developing spiritual perception of the alchemist.

Thus the outward striving of the male figures in the three realms of alchemy unite with the inner sensitivity and open receptivity of the threefold female figure, who is also necessary for the alchemist's development.

ER
GON.
CVM DEO.
PAREB
GON.
T.S.C.
Arte Nat-
ura
HINC SAPIENTIA
LABORE

Mandala Nine.

MANDALA GROUP TEN

In this alchemical mandala group are shown three versions of the same mandala form found in Andreas Libavius' *Commentariorum Alchymiae*, Frankfurt, 1606. These three engravings illustrate different ways of presenting the essence of a mandala, and afford us an excellent opportunity to see the inner workings of the mandala. They are also particularly interesting in that they tie together many of the symbolic threads of bird symbolism explored in the commentary to Mandala Thirteen.

MANDALA A

This is described in the text as an emblem of Heinrich Kuhdorfer and is assigned a date of 1421 by Libavius. The text includes a minute description which is quoted below, as it describes various colors to be associated with parts of the illustration:

> A. A small charcoal fire under the glass.
>
> B. This space is filled by a winged serpent with a long tail, wearing a crown like the fabulous basilisk. It lies on its back with its feet in the air, and bites its tail, which is doubled back, thus being the dragon which is said to eat its own tail. It is of horrible appearance, green in color, with a grey or ashy tail.
>
> C. Here an eagle is to be painted with saffron feet and beak, wings outspread, many colored plumage in the wings, body and tail, some feathers being white, others black, green, yellow, as in a picture of the peacock's tail, or the rainbow.
>
> D. In the field, a black crow.
>
> E. A red rose on a silver field.
>
> F. A white rose on a red field.
>
> G. A maiden's head, silver, representing the Moon.
>
> H. A lion's head, gold, representing the Sun.
>
> I. One red rose on a silver field.
>
> K. A saffron-colored candle.
>
> L. Three gold stars on a silver field.
>
> M. Six dark blue stars on a golden field.
>
> N. A white or silver candle, may also be saffron-colored.
>
> O. Three white roses on a red field.
>
> P. A king holding red- or blood-colored lilies in his hand.
>
> Q. The king's wife or mother holding white or silver lilies.
>
> R. A silver candle.

V
X
V
X
V
T
I
K
L
R
S
M
N
P
Q
G
H
F
E
D
C
B

MANDALA TEN: VERSION A.

S. A red candle.

T. A plate of a crown, gold.

V. Candles in an apple.

X. Gold and silver lilies.

MANDALA B

One can see that this mandala is a much more elaborate version of the former and a detailed description of it also occurs in Libavius' text. He describes each detail as follows:

A. A pediment or foundation, like the earth.

B. Two giants or Atlases, resting on the foundations, who, to the left and right, hold up a globe on their shoulders and prop it with their hands.

C. A four-headed dragon, breathing forth, upwards towards the globe, four stages of fire; from one mouth there must come, as it were, air; from the second, thin smoke; from the third, smoke with fire; from the fourth, pure fire.

D. Mercury with a silver chain; beside him, two beasts bound with the chain and crouching.

E. A green lion.

F. A dragon crowned, single-headed. These two beasts mean the same thing, namely, the mercurial liquid which is the first matter of the stone.

G. A three-headed silver eagle, two heads drooping and, as it were, fading, while from the third it must pour forth white water or the mercurial liquid into the place of the sea, marked H.

I. A picture of a wind (god) blowing downward to the sea beneath.

K. The picture of a red lion, from whose breast is to flow red blood into the sea beneath, which must be so colored as to seem a mixture of gold and silver, or of red and white.

L. An expanse of black water, as in chaos: there is signified (thereby) putrefaction. From this emerges a sort of mountain, black at the base, white at the summit, with an overflow of white streaming down from the summit. For it is the symbol of the first solution and coagulation, and again of the second solution.

M. The aforesaid mountain.

N. Black heads of crows looking out from the sea.

O. A silver rain falling from clouds onto the summit of the mountain, whereby is figured, firstly, the nutrition and ablution of Lato by Azoth; secondly, the second solution, whereby the element of air is brought forth from earth and water. Earth is the appearance of the mountain; water is that first liquid of the sea.

V
X
X
S
S
R
R
P
P
M
M
N
N
K
G
H
H
D
E
B
B
C
A

Mandala Ten: Version B.

P. The shape of clouds, from which comes dew, or rain, and the nutritive liquid.

Q. The form of the sky, in which must lie a dragon, on his back, eating his own tail; this is the image of the second coagulation.

R. A negro and a negress, holding up two globes, above and to the side of them. They are supported by a larger globe, and signify the blackness of the second operation, in the second putrefaction.

S. Here let there be represented a sea of pure silver, which typifies the mercurial liquid, the medium by which the tinctures are connected.

T. Here paint a swan swimming on the sea and spewing out of its mouth a white fluid. This swan is the white elixir, the white chalk, the arsenic of the philosophers, common to both ferments. It should support on its back and wings a globe placed above it.

V. An eclipse of the sun.

X. The sun rising from the sea, that is from the mercurial water, into which also the elixir must pass. Thereupon comes forth the real eclipse of the sun. On either side of it should be painted a rainbow, to indicate the Peacock's Tail, which then appears in the coagulation.

Y. An eclipse of the moon, which should also have a rainbow at the sides, and near the rainbow part of the sea for the moon to sink into; this is the symbol of the white fermentation. The sea in both pictures should be a little dark.

Z. The moon sinking into the sea.

a. A king, in a purple robe, with a gold crown, having a lion standing beside him.

b. A queen, decorated with a silver crown, stroking a white or silver eagle which perches beside her. In one hand the queen should carry a white lily, the king a red lily.

c. A phoenix perched on a glove and burning itself; from the ashes must fly a number of birds silver and golden. For this is the symbol of augmentation and multiplication.

MANDALA C

This mandala expresses the alchemical process of development along a vertical axis. There is a definite fourfoldness to the lower part of the mandala: this is evidenced by the two 'Atlas'-like supporters and the two figures resting upon the upper part of the globe. These four figures in turn support the upper part of the mandala, which is more threefold in essence. There is a solidity about the lower part of the mandala; indeed, this is emphasized by its being supported by the Atlas figures kneeling upon a rectangular base. The upper part is more an equilibrium of disparate elements, represented by the three globes which are held together in a balance. So the key to this mandala is a

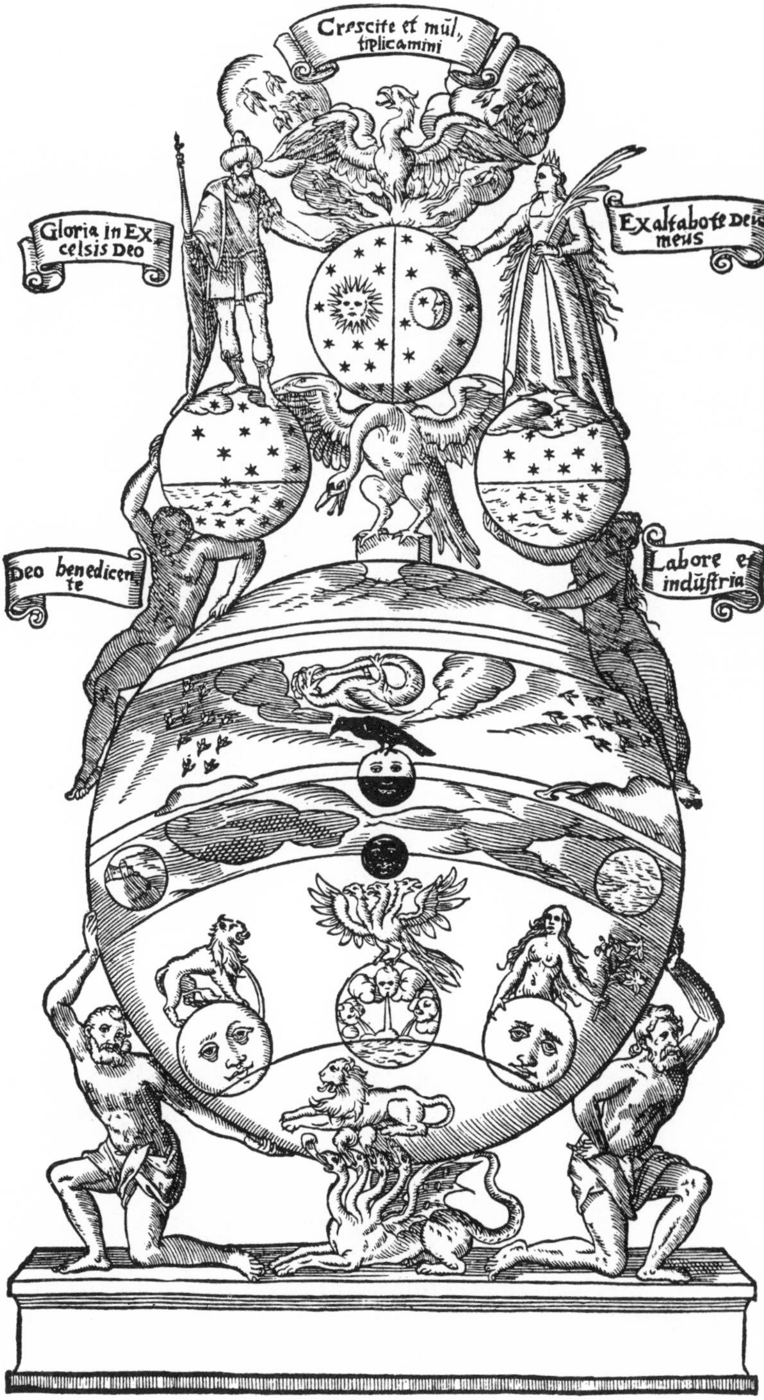
Crescite et mul, tiplicamini
Gloria in Ex celsis Deo
Exaltabote Deus meus
Deo benedicente
Labore et industria

MANDALA TEN: VERSION C.

transformation from the fourfold to the threefold, from the Four Elements to the Three Principles. Both of these facets of the mandala process are subdivided into a series of stages in which polarities are experienced and symbolized by various animal forms, and by bird forms in particular.

At the bottom of the spherical vessel in which the transformation of the Elements occurs, a four-headed dragon energizes the process through the four degrees of heat—Earth of Fire, Water of Fire, Air of Fire, and Fire of Fire.

Within this vessel one can recognize three distinct layers. In the lowest layer certain polarities express themselves in a separation of the archetypal Sun and Moon forces. These are symbolized by the Sun with the Lion standing upon it, and by the Moon with the Virgin upon it. The Red Blood of the Lion pours into the Sun disc, while the Moon disc is nourished by white lilies, symbolic perhaps of the White Milk of the Virgin. These two discs are balanced by a central sphere in which three cherubs mingle their forces, so it is essential that this polarity must be balanced by the third element. This balance is seen vertically in the symbols of the triple-headed Eagle above and Lion below. The Gluten of the Eagle and the Green Lion is also a component of the *conjunctio*. Thus we have a quaternity, polarized into a duality, but united in a triplicity, forming the first inner stage of the process. At the boundary of this stage and the next we see an eclipsed Sun, and when we remember that an eclipse of the Sun is a conjunction of the Sun and Moon—the Moon covering the Sun disc—we will recognize this as a suitable symbol for the conclusion of the first Conjunction.

The next stage involves a working through Air and Water as the two circular inserts on the left and right respectively indicate. This is a period of Putrefaction or *nigredo*—a phase of outer blackening during which an inner evolution of forces is free to occur. At the conclusion of this stage of the process we see the bird symbol of the Nigredo, the Black Crow or Raven, surmounting the Sun-Moon globe which is just coming out of eclipse.

This final stage of the first part of the process involves a separation-conjunction cycle, which is indicated by the ascending birds on the right and the descending birds on the left. We are reminded of the detailed symbolic description of the alchemical process given in *The Crowning of Nature* manuscript (Magnum Opus Hermetic Sourceworks Number 3). Earth and Water are intimately related in this Separation and Conjunction and we note that, as the birds ascend from the land, water is expelled into the ocean. Moreover, as the birds descend in the conjunction phase the land seems to sink down into the water. This cyclical process of separation and conjunction reaches fruition in the Ouroboros, the snake, here in bird form as a cockerel, swallowing its own tail. This integration of the elements closes the first part of the work.

The alchemist now possesses the integrated substance of the work, the Philosophical Mercury, one might say. And now he must polarize this in turn to form the White and Red Tinctures. This is shown above in the three globes. The dark male and female figures supporting the two globes represent the unperfected polarization, but when this is brought together in the third globe, which is dual solar/lunar, the true archetypal polarities can appear as the King and Queen. From these two tinctures of Sun and Moon are evolved the Phoenix and the White Swan. The Phoenix, representing the solar fire tincture, is shown on its pyre in a state of resurrection; the White Swan, representing the lunar, earthly tincture, stands upon the Cube of the Earth. In the realm of the soul these tinctures represent processes which color the astral body or aura of the operator.

While all three mandalas incorporate the same process—though they approach it through different symbolic sequences—the experienced student of alchemy should be able to find the key to the integration of these symbolic descriptions. It is an essential task in the inner digestion of alchemical truths to be able to recognize the same process described in different symbolic patterns, even though these outer symbolic descriptions may be inconsistent and mutually incompatible. Thus the student of alchemical symbolism often faces paradox in the outer symbols, but is led to an inner grasp of some alchemical truth.

MANDALA ELEVEN

This engraving of Matthieu Merian first appeared in J. Daniel Mylius' *Philosophia Reformata* of 1622, though it is more familiar from its reprinting in the *Musaeum Hermeticum* of 1625. It shows us a mandala centered upon the Tree of the Soul, beneath which an old philosopher is instructing a young knight. They raise their left hands in greeting, indicating the esoteric purpose of their meeting (the left being the 'sinister' side of mystical and hidden things). This philosopher is the Wise Old Man within us all, while the Young Man is the explorative, investigative aspect of the soul that seeks enlightenment and quests after the wisdom of the spirit. The Old Man leans upon a staff, representing his long experience, while the Young Man, as if a knight on the quest, bears a sword, a weapon of the intellect, to arm him on his exploration.

Between these two figures stands the Soul Tree, bearing the Sun, Moon and the five planets. This is the realm which the being of the alchemist must penetrate, the seven spheres of the planetary forces in the soul which he must traverse and integrate. He must also bring together the King and Queen archetypes of the male and female forces in the soul, as well as the Four Elements: Earth, and the Fire breathing salamander, on the left; and Water, and Air represented by the bird, on the right.

Around the Tree we see the most important aspect of this mandala, a representation of the inner process which takes place in seven stages:

The **first stage** is a death/*nigredo* where the soul bird is seen perched upon a skull. Thus a death/*nigredo* stands at the beginning of the work, and a separation occurs between the soul and the body in the process.

At the **second stage** the soul bird gazes at its reflection in the dead earth realm. Through the *nigredo*, those facets of the husk of the old soul forces that have died are transformed and mirror back to the soul an essence of its being.

In the **third stage**, two soul birds descend and begin to raise the dead essence of the soul in the form of the bird corpse. They raise the essence of the soul that is anchored in the earth realm towards the higher spiritual realm.

At the **fourth stage** a turning point is reached when the dead corpse of the soul element, anchored in the earth realm, is spiritualized into a crown. The soul birds which can soar within the alchemist's being to the highest spiritual sphere are useless to his consciousness unless they can incarnate this spirit in a material form. Here they have transformed the dead skull of the first stage, through the bird-corpse, into a crown. This crown is brought into the lower regions of the soul by the polarized forces of the two soul birds that have been operating through this central part of the process.

Mandala Eleven.

During the **fifth stage** it is planted in the earth of the soul and begins to grow. Here the spiritual potentialities in the crown begin to reveal themselves as a living presence in the soul.

The **sixth stage** sees the formation of the two Soul Tinctures, the Red (Solar) Tincture represented by the rose blossoms, and the White (Lunar) Tincture represented by the Unicorn. These tinctures or Stones are the permanent incarnation within the soul of the archetypal spiritual energies.

Finally, the **seventh stage** is reached with the resurrection of the body, here seen as a female figure. The alchemist returns to full consciousness in the body, bearing within the essence of the process. As this passive weaving of these tinctures into the being of the alchemist reflects a feminine aspect of the process, the alchemist is represented in female form. We note the polarities of the stages:

Four: The Elevation to the Spirit and creation of the Crown

Three: the raising of the corpse	↔	Five: descent and planting of the seed
Two: the mirroring of the soul	↔	Six: the Soul Tinctures
One: the Death/Nigredo	↔	Seven: the Resurrection

MANDALA TWELVE

The Temple of Pansophia from the *Compass of the Wise,* a late 18th century German alchemical text, is a mandala bringing together the two Kabbalistic columns (also known as the Masonic Columns) with alchemical ideas.

Through the pillars Joachin and Boaz, the alchemist gazes upon the meeting of the heavenly forces of the celestial realm with the vessels of the earthly world of substance. He must place his consciousness at the meeting point of these two streams and fulfil the Hermetic maxim, uniting that which is above with that which is below. The alchemist must inwardly perform a middle pillar exercise if he is to balance the two energies of the columns. Joachin is the male, active, fire (Aesch) column with the Sun at its top, while Boaz is the female, passive, water (Maim) pillar with the Moon at its top.

Above in the heavens, The Higher World, we see the realm of the fixed stars with the constellations Aries, Taurus, and Gemini, and the regions of the Sun and Moon and the planets. From these pour down influences which are focused into the archetypal Three Principles: 🜔 Salt, 🜍 Sulphur, and ☿ Mercury, which are united into a single symbol at the center, just above the line of the horizon. The Solar and Lunar energies are in turn interpreted as the Father and Mother polarities.

These spiritual energies, having been focussed in the archetype of the Three Principles, which acts like a prism, diffract out into The Lower World. There they meet a table supported by seven legs or columns bearing the signs of the seven planets, which indicate the seven metals: ☉ Gold, ☽ Silver, ☿ Mercury, ♃ Tin, ♄ Lead, ♀ Copper, and ♂ Iron. This table or mirror is the realm of substance which the lower region holds up to clothe the spiritual energies from above. From this process arise seven substances, the Metalloids, which incarnate these forces in material form. Six are shown around the circumference of the table with one, Antimony, at the center:

🜖 Vitriol		🜍 Sulphur
🜕 Saltpeter	♁ Antimony	🜿 Tartar
○ Alum		🜹 Sal Ammoniac

The alchemist must place his consciousness at the focal point of the higher forces. Then he can touch upon the upper archetype of the Three Principles and their manifestation in the substance of the metalloids. Above the archetypes of the Three Principles lies the essence of the planetary forces, while below the table/mirror of substance are seven supporting legs with funnels and vessels.

Thus the energies of the metalloids flow into the seven planetary metals of the outer and lower material world.

In an odd way, there is an electromagnetic interpretation of this mandala. The columns Joachin and Boaz have clockwise and anticlockwise helices wound around them. If we imagined the columns as electrical conductors, then a current flowing from above to below (paralleling the spiritual energies) would induce a magnetic field. The lines of force of this field on the Joachin column would run clockwise with the wreath helix. A current flowing up the Boaz column would similarly induce anticlockwise lines of magnetic force. The title of the book from which this illustration is taken is *The Compass of the Wise*, and we can further interpret the central table/mirror as a compass with a magnetic needle sensitive to such induced fields. Here the needle has oriented itself between the polarities of Sulphur and Saltpeter. This is not to suggest that the creator of this illustration knew about the existence of induced magnetic fields, as this phenomenon was not officially discovered until 1820 by Oersted, but the parallels are perhaps of interest.

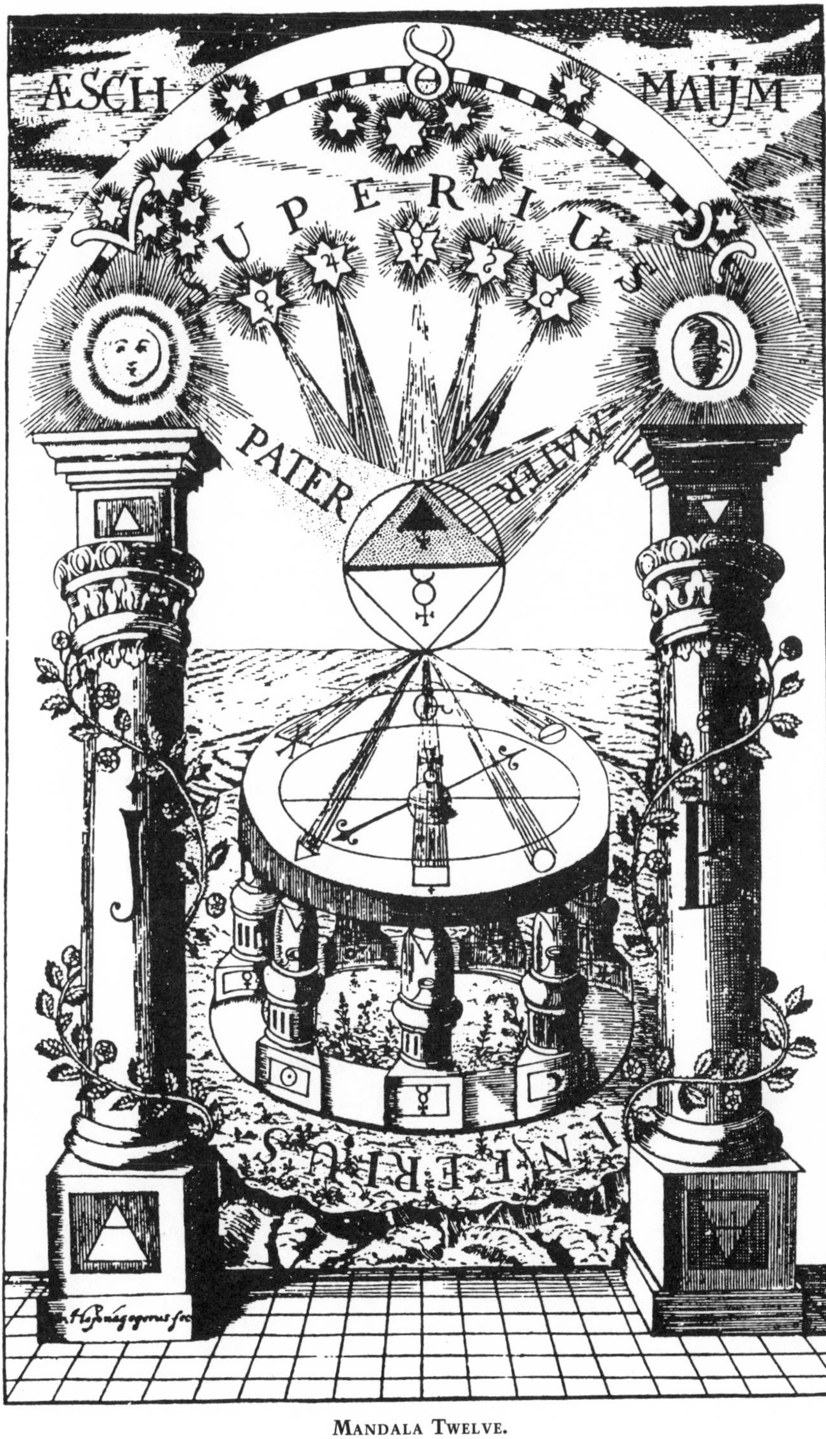
ÆSCH
MAIJM
SUPERIUS
PATER
MATER
INFERIUS

Mandala Twelve.

MANDALA THIRTEEN

This is the Ninth Key in the series of the Twelve Keys of Basil Valentine, a treatise published in the *Musaeum Hermeticum* in 1625 by Lucas Jennis, with engravings by Matthieu Merian. The mandala divides into two sections.

THE LOWER SECTION shows us three hearts out of which grow three serpents. These represent the Three Principles, Salt, Sulphur and Mercury, or the realms of Body, Soul and Spirit. The hearts are the points of centrality in these three facets, the essence of the three principles, while the snakes are the polarized expression of these principles. (As we have seen in the commentaries to other mandalas, the snake with its head and tail is a symbol of polarization.) We note also that the heart with its two chambers already possesses a tendency toward a certain polarity in its form. The three snakes in this illustration are reaching out to grasp each other's tails, which are still fused with the central hearts. Thus they begin to integrate, and we see a cycle from the essence (heart) of the Three Principles, to polarized outer expression (snakes), to the uniting of these into a wholeness again: the final form which the symbol tends towards could be pictured as something resembling a three petalled flower.

THE UPPER SECTION of this mandala is a working with the Four and the Two. We see two figures, a male and a female, in a strange position, as bottom to bottom they form a most odd cross with their heads and feet. Their arms reach out backwards to complete the form of a square. We perceive a fourfold cross-square formed out of the polarities of the male and female, and at the points of the cross we find the four alchemical birds we have often met before in these mandalas.

At the man's feet we see the BLACK CROW, at his head the PHOENIX. At the woman's feet the PEACOCK appears with resplendent tail, and at her feet the WHITE SWAN. These are symbols of the four stages in the alchemical work:

> Black Crow—Nigredo, the initial darkness or chaos into which the substance must descend in order for its further evolution to occur.
>
> Peacock's Tail—a sudden iridescence of colors that marks the beginning of integration, the formation of the Philosophical Mercury.
>
> White Swan—the preparation of the White Tincture of the Lunar forces, Philosophical Salt.
>
> The Phoenix—the preparation of the Red Tincture of the Solar forces, Philosophical Sulphur.

Mandala Thirteen.

These four birds are also connected with the elements:

Black Crow - Earth
White Swan - Water
Peacock's Tail - Air
Phoenix - Fire

These bird symbols, being related to the masculine and feminine figures, form certain interesting polarities. The Black Crow is thus opposed to the Peacock's Tail stage, and the White Swan (White Tincture) is polarized with the Phoenix (Red Tincture). However, another set of relationships is created through connecting the head and feet of the figures: the masculine polarity, moving from the feet to the head of the male figure, leads the Black Crow to the Phoenix; the feminine polarity, progressing from feet to head, shows an evolution of the Peacock's Tail into the White Swan.

This mandala symbolizes the integration which may occur through experiencing the alchemical polarities. These polarities include the Three Principles, the masculine and the feminine, and the four stages of the alchemical process, which are seen polarized in different permutations.

MANDALA FOURTEEN

This mandala is found as a figure in a mid-seventeenth century manuscript translation of George Ripley's *Marrow of Alchemy* in the British Library (Ms. Sloane 3667).

This mandala takes the form of a Tree of the Soul and shows the interweaving of two archetypal energies along a vertical axis. The essence of this figure would appear to parallel the Eastern esotericism of *chakras*, centers of subtle energy, found along the spine. These chakras in Eastern esotericism are described as having currents of soul energy, the Ida (lunar) and Pingala (solar) Nadis, entwined around them, and a central channel, the Sushumna, wherein moves the kundalini energy. This mandala pictures this archetypal reality in alchemical terms.

At the bottom of the illustration we see a horseshoe-shaped form, like the pelvic bones in man. This is the site of the basal chakra, the *muladhara*. It has four roots, and bears four growths (2 leaves and 2 fruits). Two of its roots lie in the Corpus (body) and two in the Spiritus (spirit). Thus the roots of the soul tree take their nourishment both from our bodily and spiritual natures. Another two roots twine around the symbol of Mercury, the living Quicksilver of the Soul, the kundalini energy, and these roots reach down into the Lead of the Philosophers, the deep dark realm of the unconscious forces and impulses in the soul. This quixotic Mercury, paradoxically uniting the lunar ☽ , solar ☉ and earthly + —the spiritual and the material—is also pictured by another ambivalent substance, Antimony, the metal which is also a non-metal (a metalloid). The four petals of the *muladhara* are represented by two fruits—the Gluten of the White Eagle, and the Red Lion—and by the two leaves which bear the soluble flowing aspect of these archetypes—the Solution of the Eagle's Gluten, and the Solution of the Blood of the Red Lion. These are the two soul tinctures of the lunar and solar currents, the incarnation of these soul energies in soul substance; the Gluten of the Eagle corresponds to the Ida (lunar) energies, and the Blood of the Red Lion to the Pingala (solar) energies.

These two energies are polarized in the *muladhara* but become united in the next and higher chakra, the sexual center (in Eastern esotericism, the *svadishthana* chakra), and we see this alchemically as the Conjunction. Through alchemy we can find both the male and female, solar and lunar currents in our beings, and our sexual center is an area of our being where both of these two currents can be inwardly united.

The next chakra is the Heart Center (*anahata* chakra), the central organ of this line of chakras in the soul. It is the site of the Philosophers' Stone (the

LAPIS). If the Stone is incarnated in the center of the Soul, it provides a solid foundation upon which to build the subtle architecture of our inner being.

Above this we find the Throat Chakra (*visuddha*) in which lies the alchemical FERMENT. This is that subtle substance which brings creative life into the soul forces. It provides the seething, bubbling, creatively outgoing energies of the soul. This is incarnated in our human voice, in our word organ, which is the main channel for our creative expression. However, this alchemical ferment also energizes other levels of creative work.

Above this is the TINCTURE, which resides in the Brow Center. This, the two petalled lotus (*ajna* chakra) of Eastern esotericism, integrates the two soul currents Ida and Pingala. As we see in this figure, the two trunks of the soul tree finally fuse together at this point. This Brow Chakra is the seat of the soul of an enlightened human being, who thus has the ability to tincture all he touches with his soul.

Finally, the Crown at the top of the diagram corresponds to the Crown Chakra (*sahasrara*), the soul organ through which the enlightened being perceives and unites with the Macrocosm, thus uniting the Cosmic with the inner potential of the Earthly, the PHILOSOPHIC LEAD

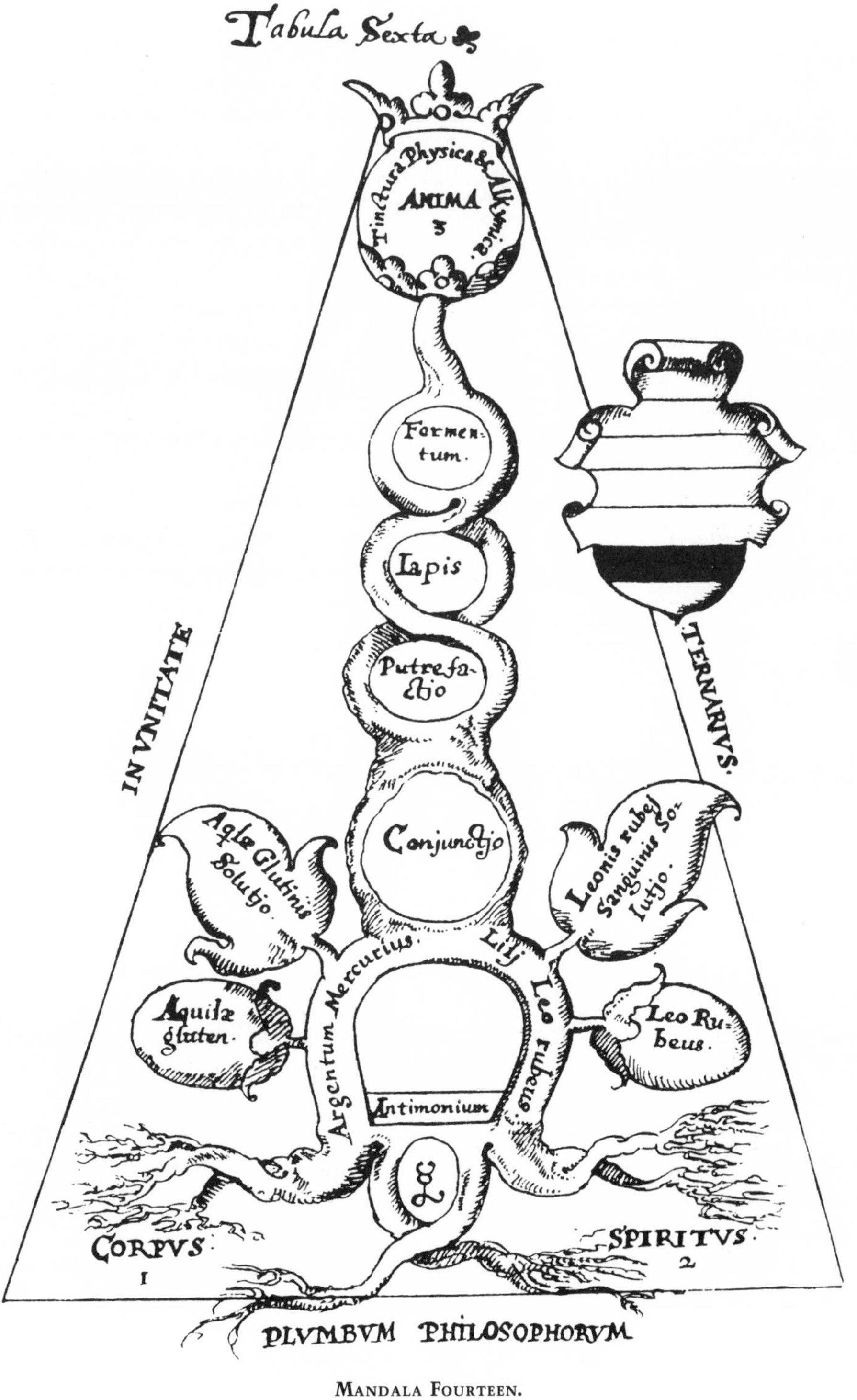
Tabula Sexta
Tinctura Physica & Alkymica.
ANIMA
Fermentum.
Lapis
Putrefactio
Conjunctio
Aqlæ Glutinis Solutio.
Leonis rubei Sanguinis Solutio.
Argentum Mercurius.
Lilij
Leo rubeus.
Aquilæ gluten.
Leo Rubeus.
Antimonium
IN UNITATE
TERNARIUS.
CORPUS
1
SPIRITUS
2
PLUMBUM PHILOSOPHORUM

MANDALA FOURTEEN.

MANDALA FIFTEEN

This mandala is from *The Secret Symbols of the Rosicrucians*, the *Geheime Figuren*, published at Altona, 1785 (Plate 1), and is also found in the D.O.M.A. manuscript in the collection of Manly Palmer Hall (Plate 2). It is relatively late, being dated to the end of the 18th century. However, the roots of the ideas contained within it originate back in the late 16th and early 17th century alchemical symbolist tradition. This work should therefore be seen as a late synthesis of this tradition and, like the other mandalas from this compilation, it is a detailed representation of the Rosicrucian alchemist's view of the forces bound up in creation, and their emanation through the process of the spiritual evolution of the Cosmos.

It should be read starting from the top, from the Eternal Uncreated, pictured as a spherical radiance, through the six-pointed star of the First Creation. Below it is another spherical realm, that of the Primordial Hyle, which eventually separates into the realms of Light and Nature, the Above and the Below, the external and the internal. Now that this separation has occurred between Substance and Essence, it is the task of humanity to reunite these opposite tendencies, and this process is shown in the lower part of the mandala, presented symbolically in the form of a complex six-pointed star.

We will now look at each of these realms, these stages of emanation, in turn.

The first realm, the Uncreated, from which the creation emanates, is the realm of the Eternal Sun wrapped in its Divine Nature and Power.

The Triune God rests in this center and will come out from this center. This Eternal Uncreated Nature at the center bears within it the germ of the three persons in God, shown as the three circles around the center: the innermost is 'Geist,' Spirit, 'the Eternal Quintessence'; then 'Gott,' God, the Primal Material of God or 'First Substance'; then the Word, the 'three principles in one essence.' The outer part of the circle shows God's Spirit, God's Life and God's Light, the Divine Fire, all of which find expression in humanity.

The Eternal, Invisible Heavenly Trinity of Spirit, Word, and God, each, through the Divine Fiat, emanate a syzygy—the Temporal, Visible Earthly Holy Trinity—the Father corresponding to God, the Holy Ghost corresponding to the Spirit, and the Son corresponding to the Word. At this stage in spiritual evolution Nature and Time are born from Eternity. This is the meaning of the radiant six-pointed star, the union of the heavenly pointing trinity and the earthly pointing trinity.

This stage still exists on a higher spiritual plane, not having descended far from the high spiritual level of the Uncreated sphere. It contains the Alpha and

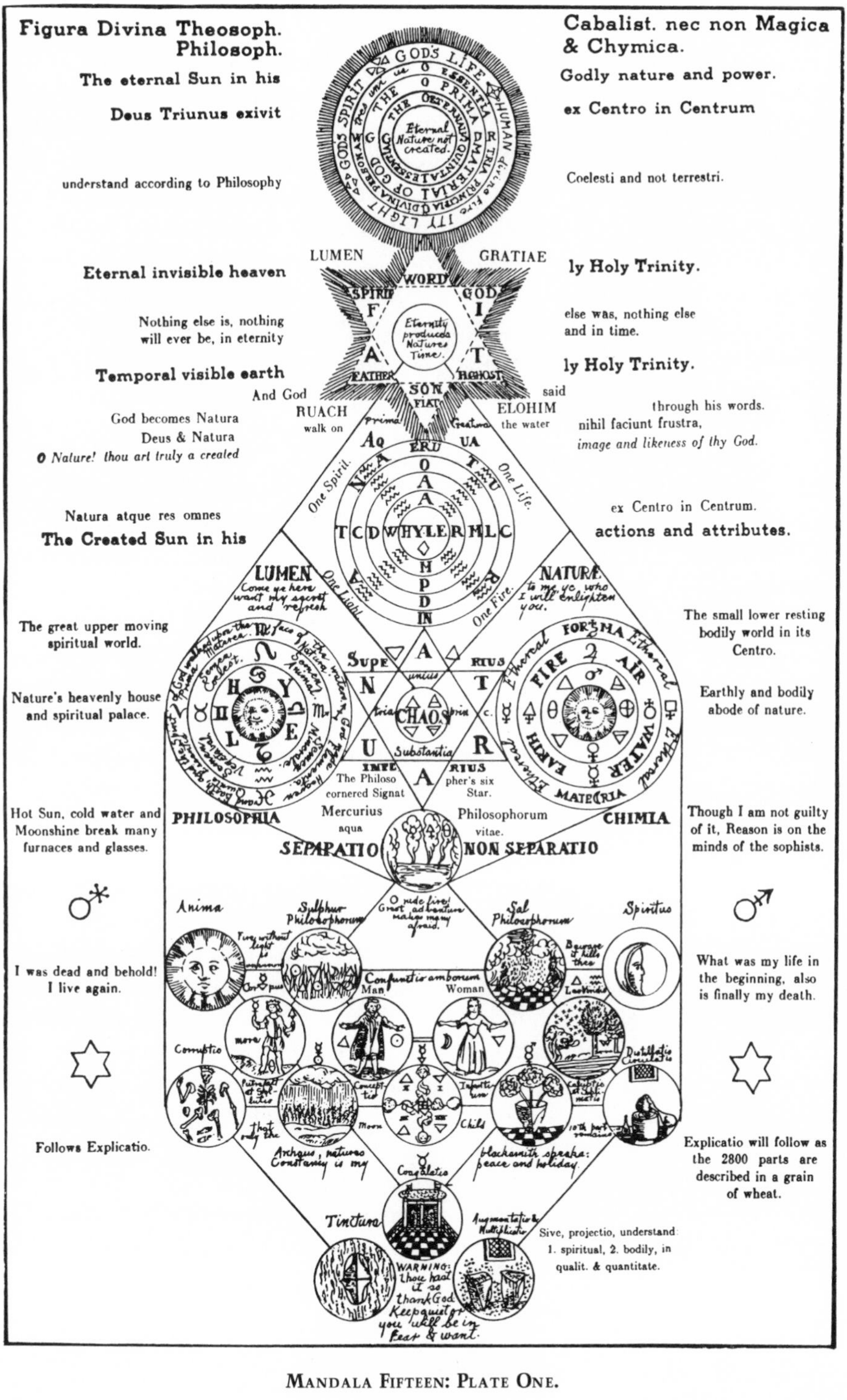
Figura Divina Theosoph. Philosoph.
Cabalist. nec non Magica & Chymica.
The eternal Sun in his
Godly nature and power.
Deus Triunus exivit
ex Centro in Centrum
understand according to Philosophy
Coelesti and not terrestri.
Eternal Nature not created.
LUMEN
GRATIAE
Eternal invisible heaven
ly Holy Trinity.
WORD
SPIRIT
GOD
FATHER
H.GHOST
SON
FIAT
Eternity produces Natures Time.
Nothing else is, nothing will ever be, in eternity
else was, nothing else and in time.
Temporal visible earth
ly Holy Trinity.
And God
said
RUACH
ELOHIM
walk on
the water
through his words.
God becomes Natura
Deus & Natura
nihil faciunt frustra,
O Nature! thou art truly a created
image and likeness of thy God.
One Spirit.
One Life.
HYLE
Natura atque res omnes
ex Centro in Centrum.
The Created Sun in his
actions and attributes.
LUMEN
NATURE
One Light.
One Fire.
The great upper moving spiritual world.
The small lower resting bodily world in its Centro.
Nature's heavenly house and spiritual palace.
Earthly and bodily abode of nature.
CHAOS
Substantia
The Philoso phers six cornered Signat Star.
FIRE
AIR
WATER
EARTH
MATERIA
Hot Sun, cold water and Moonshine break many furnaces and glasses.
PHILOSOPHIA
Mercurius aqua
Philosophorum vitae.
CHIMIA
Though I am not guilty of it, Reason is on the minds of the sophists.
SEPARATIO
NON SEPARATIO
Anima
Sulphur Philosophorum
Sal Philosophorum
Spiritus
I was dead and behold! I live again.
Man
Woman
What was my life in the beginning, also is finally my death.
Corruptio
Child
Moon
Follows Explicatio.
Explicatio will follow as the 2800 parts are described in a grain of wheat.
Coagulatio
Tinctura
Sive, projectio, understand: 1. spiritual, 2. bodily, in qualit. & quantitate.
WARNING: thou hast it so thank God. Keep quiet or you will be in fear & want.

Mandala Fifteen: Plate One.

the Omega, the beginning and end of creation. In Eternity "Nothing else is, nothing else was, and nothing else will ever be."

Now the Spirit takes a step into more material embodiment. The Ruach Elohim, the Breath of God of the First Creation, depicted as the radiant six-pointed star, hovers above the waters. This is the realm of Hyle, the primordial root substance (the *mulaprakriti* of Eastern esotericism), shown in the circular symbol contained within the square of the quaternary, One Spirit - One Life - One Light - One Fire. The quaternary of Spirit, Life, Light and Fire mirrors the eternal uncreated realm. The primordial substance of Hyle has four qualities—warmth, dampness, cold , and dryness—as dimensions of its being, and these at a later stage of evolution create the archetypes of the four elements. Thus, the realm of Nature is born, created in the pattern and likeness of God (the Eternal Uncreated).

A further stage of descent occurs in the next part of the figure, in which another separation takes place. It is symbolized by the interlaced triangles of a six-pointed star at the center of this mandala. Now that the spiritual essence has been committed to and united with Hyle, the primordial substance, a densification occurs and Hyle becomes Chaos. Through this densification, a separation comes about between a superior world and an inferior world.

These two are shown as the two spherical universes on the left and right. On the left we have the upper, great, moveable, spiritual world. This is Nature's heavenly residence and spiritual palace. On the right the lower, small, latent and corporeal world contains in its center Nature's earthly abode and corporeal palace. The upper world is the realm of the stars, as we see the zodiacal signs on the three rings of the diagrammatic representation. This is the realm of the creative archetypes,"God created Heaven and Earth, and the Spirit of God was suspended above the Waters." The creative archetypes emanate the spiritual essences of human seed, animal seed, vegetable seed, and the seed of the minerals. The lower world is the realm of the planets and the elements. These receive the archetypal forces of the upper realm and weave them into substance through the activity of the Ethers. Both of these are centered upon the Created Sun. This is the Sun in its natural rather than spiritual embodiment, who through these activities and attributes is the center of all creation. This Created Sun is the lower manifestation of the Uncreated Sun of the highest realm of our mandala.

The Philosophers' six-pointed star at the center of nature is the point of separation and unity between the above and the below, between Form and Matter, Essence and Substance. The spiritual archetype has here descended into the four elements, and there arises therefrom the Three Principles in One

DIVINE FIGURE OF THEOSOPHY: CABALA: NOT ONLY MAGIC AND PHILOSOPHY, BUT ALSO CHEMISTRY

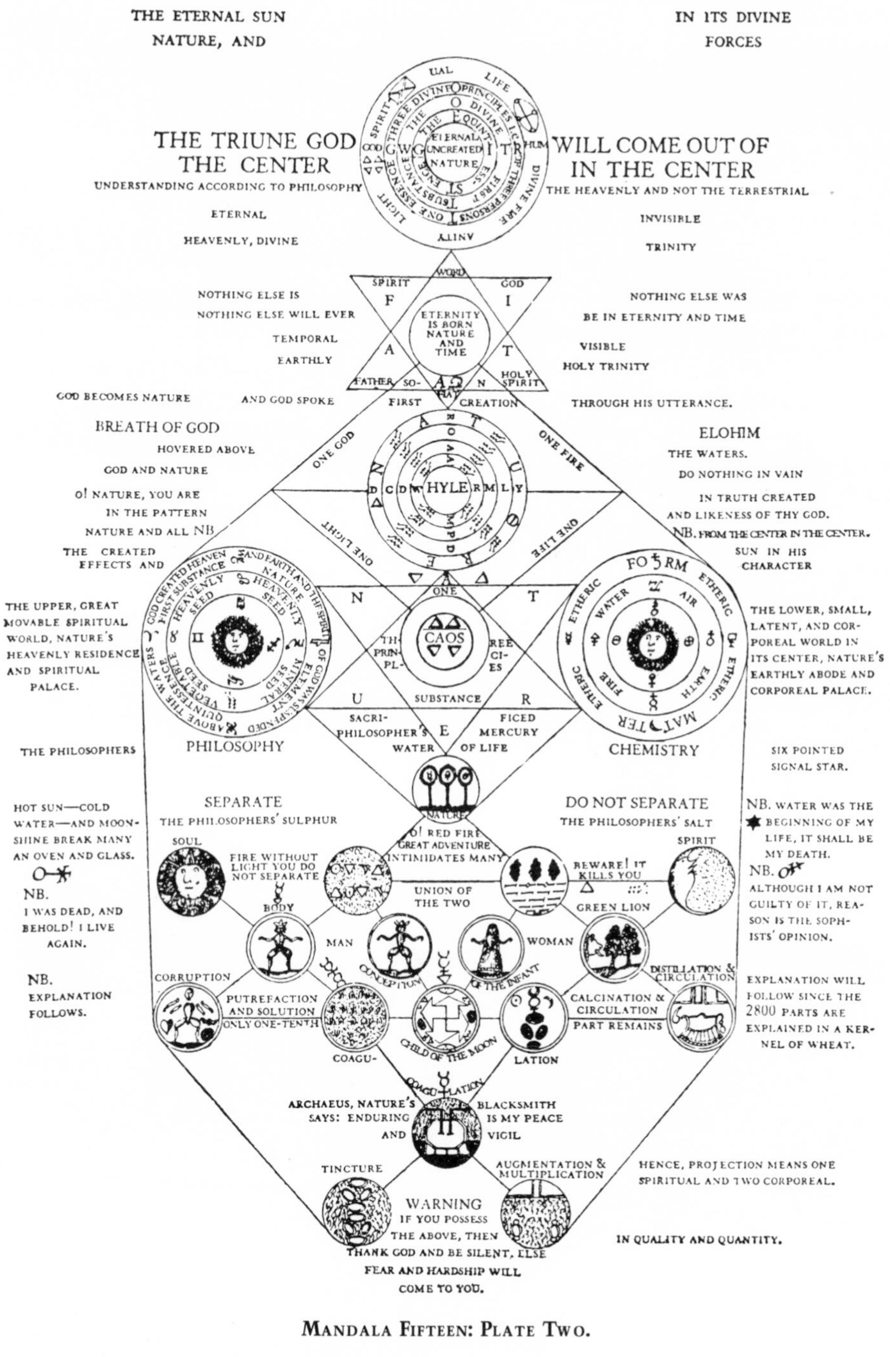
THE ETERNAL SUN
NATURE, AND
IN ITS DIVINE
FORCES
THE TRIUNE GOD
THE CENTER
UNDERSTANDING ACCORDING TO PHILOSOPHY
ETERNAL
HEAVENLY, DIVINE
WILL COME OUT OF
IN THE CENTER
THE HEAVENLY AND NOT THE TERRESTRIAL
INVISIBLE
TRINITY
ETERNAL UNCREATED NATURE
WORD
SPIRIT
GOD
F
I
A
T
ETERNITY IS BORN NATURE AND TIME
FATHER
SO-
N
HOLY SPIRIT
NOTHING ELSE IS
NOTHING ELSE WILL EVER
TEMPORAL
EARTHLY
NOTHING ELSE WAS
BE IN ETERNITY AND TIME
VISIBLE
HOLY TRINITY
GOD BECOMES NATURE
AND GOD SPOKE
FIRST
CREATION
THROUGH HIS UTTERANCE.
BREATH OF GOD
HOVERED ABOVE
GOD AND NATURE
O! NATURE, YOU ARE
IN THE PATTERN
NATURE AND ALL NB
THE CREATED
EFFECTS AND
ELOHIM
THE WATERS.
DO NOTHING IN VAIN
IN TRUTH CREATED
AND LIKENESS OF THY GOD.
NB. FROM THE CENTER IN THE CENTER.
SUN IN HIS
CHARACTER
ONE GOD
ONE FIRE
ONE LIGHT
ONE LIFE
HYLE
ONE
CAOS
N
T
TH-
PRIN-
PL-
REE
CI-
ES
U
SUBSTANCE
R
SACRI-
PHILOSOPHER'S
WATER
E
FICED
MERCURY
OF LIFE
THE UPPER, GREAT
MOVABLE SPIRITUAL
WORLD, NATURE'S
HEAVENLY RESIDENCE
AND SPIRITUAL
PALACE.
PHILOSOPHY
FO RM
ETHERIC
WATER
AIR
FIRE
EARTH
MAT TER
CHEMISTRY
THE LOWER, SMALL,
LATENT, AND COR-
POREAL WORLD IN
ITS CENTER, NATURE'S
EARTHLY ABODE AND
CORPOREAL PALACE.
THE PHILOSOPHERS
SIX POINTED
SIGNAL STAR.
NATURE
SEPARATE
THE PHILOSOPHERS' SULPHUR
DO NOT SEPARATE
THE PHILOSOPHERS' SALT
HOT SUN—COLD
WATER—AND MOON-
SHINE BREAK MANY
AN OVEN AND GLASS.
NB.
I WAS DEAD, AND
BEHOLD! I LIVE
AGAIN.
NB.
EXPLANATION
FOLLOWS.
NB. WATER WAS THE
BEGINNING OF MY
LIFE, IT SHALL BE
MY DEATH.
NB.
ALTHOUGH I AM NOT
GUILTY OF IT, REA-
SON IS THE SOPH-
ISTS' OPINION.
SOUL
SPIRIT
O! RED FIRE
GREAT ADVENTURE
INTIMIDATES MANY
FIRE WITHOUT
LIGHT YOU DO
NOT SEPARATE
BEWARE! IT
KILLS YOU
UNION OF
THE TWO
BODY
GREEN LION
MAN
WOMAN
CONCEPTION
OF THE INFANT
CORRUPTION
DISTILLATION &
CIRCULATION
PUTREFACTION
AND SOLUTION
ONLY ONE-TENTH
CALCINATION &
CIRCULATION
PART REMAINS
EXPLANATION WILL
FOLLOW SINCE THE
2800 PARTS ARE
EXPLAINED IN A KER-
NEL OF WHEAT.
COAGU-
CHILD OF THE MOON
LATION
COAGU-LATION
ARCHAEUS, NATURE'S
SAYS: ENDURING
AND
BLACKSMITH
IS MY PEACE
VIGIL
TINCTURE
AUGMENTATION &
MULTIPLICATION
HENCE, PROJECTION MEANS ONE
SPIRITUAL AND TWO CORPOREAL.
IN QUALITY AND QUANTITY.
WARNING
IF YOU POSSESS
THE ABOVE, THEN
THANK GOD AND BE SILENT, ELSE
FEAR AND HARDSHIP WILL
COME TO YOU.

MANDALA FIFTEEN: PLATE TWO.

substance. From this, through the operations of PHILOSOPHY and CHEMISTRY, the essence which has been now woven into substance can be revealed and activated again. Thus the lowest part of our central six-pointed star touches upon the realm of the PHILOSOPHERS' MERCURY, and out of this all the work of the alchemical evolution of substance will follow.

The lowest section of our mandala is in the form of a complex six-pointed star with various alchemical operations placed upon the vertices. Through contemplating this arrangement of symbols, we will find the key to the alchemical work which man must undertake to ennoble matter, to spiritualize it, and bring it into the state of a tincture.

At the top we have a triangular arrangement of the Three Principles, SULPHUR and SALT radiating out from the universal MERCURY OF THE PHILOSOPHERS. These link with the outer vertices ANIMA (Soul) and SPIRITUS, which bear the solar and lunar archetypes. They find their completion in the third vertex of this downward pointing large triangle which is at the bottom of the figure and is labeled COAGULATION, and which forms the basis for the completion of the work:

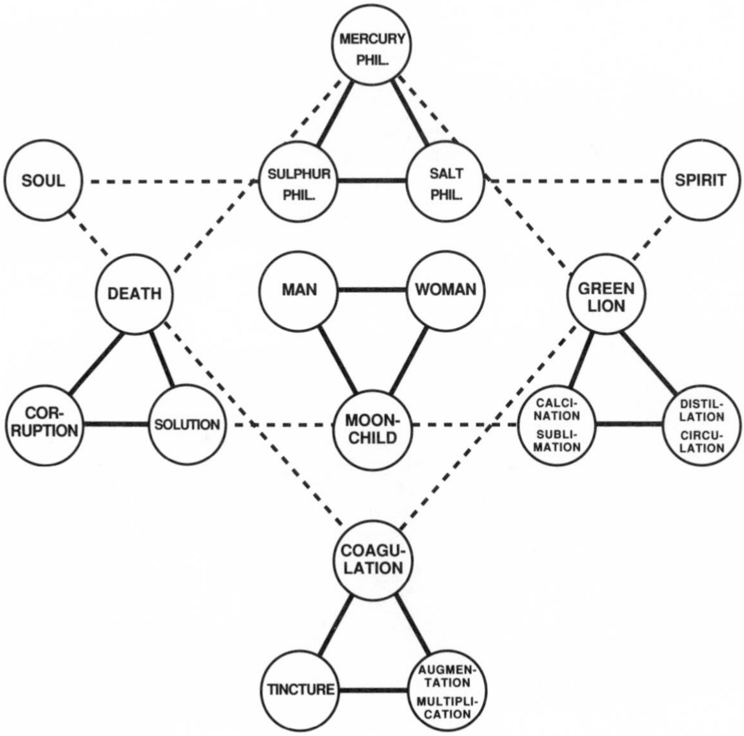
MERCURY PHIL.
SOUL
SULPHUR PHIL.
SALT PHIL.
SPIRIT
DEATH
MAN
WOMAN
GREEN LION
COR-RUPTION
SOLUTION
MOON-CHILD
CALCI-NATION SUBLI-MATION
DISTIL-LATION CIRCU-LATION
COAGU-LATION
TINCTURE
AUGMEN-TATION MULTIPLI-CATION

This diagram breaks down into four further sets of triangular arrangements, mirroring the three principles at various stages in the process. Below Anima we see a triangle formed of DEATH—CORRUPTION—SOLUTION. This is the beginning of the work, the *nigredo* of the *prima materia*. Then follows an inverted triangle at the center of the figure MAN—WOMAN—MOONCHILD, the Conception, the sowing of the seed in the *prima materia*. The Moonchild incorporates the four elements in a spiritualized form. Following this we note under the Spiritus side GREEN LION—CALCINATION AND SUBLIMATION—DISTILLATION AND CIRCULATION. These are the processes through which the spiritual essence is woven into substance.

Finally, below, we see the product of the Solar and Lunar forces from the previous stages which are fused together in a COAGULATION, out of which arises the TINCTURE and its AUGMENTATION AND MULTIPLICATION.

Thus we have in this sketch an outline of the alchemical work that we, in our unique place in the scheme of things as humans, must perform upon matter, thereby raising it to the stage of a spiritual Tincture. Meditation on this mandala will develop an inner perception of our involvement in the process of the spiritual evolution of the material world.

MANDALA SIXTEEN

This mandala also appears as one of the figures in the famous Altona Manuscript published in 1785 under the title *Secret Symbols of the Rosicrucians*. In this work it is described as 'the Mountain of the Philosophers' and has the following description appended:

> The soul of men everywhere was lost through a fall, and the health of the body suffered through a fall, Salvation came to the human soul through IEHOVA, Jesus Christ. The bodily health is brought back through a thing not good to look at. It is hidden in this painting, the highest treasure in this world, in which is the highest medicine and the greatest parts of the riches of nature, given to us by the Lord IEHOVA. It is called *Pater metallorum*, well known to the philosopher sitting in front of the mountain-cave, easy to obtain by anybody. But the sophists in their sophistic garb, tapping on the walls, recognize him not. At the right is to be seen *Lepus*, representing the art of chemistry, marvellously white, the secrets of which with fire's heat are being explored. To the left one can see freely what the right *Clavis artis* is; one cannot be too subtle with it, like a hen hatching a chicken. In the midst of the mountain, before the door, stands a courageous Lion in all its pride, whose noble blood the monster-dragon is going to shed; throwing him into a deep grave, out of it comes forth a black raven, then called *Ianua artis*, out of that comes *Aquila alba*. Even the crystal refined in the furnace will quickly show you on inspection *Servum fugitivum*, a wonder-child to many artists. The one effecting all this is *Principium laboris*. On the right in the barrel are *Sol* and *Luna*, the intelligence of the firmament. The Senior plants in it *Rad. Rubeam and Albam*. Now you proceed with constancy and *Arbor artis* appears to you, with its blossoms it announces now *Lapidem philosophorum*. Over all, the crown of the glory, ruling over all treasures.

This mandala is in the form of a Mountain of Initiation which the initiate has to ascend through various stages. The mountain itself is surrounded by a stout brickwork wall having one arched-over entrance; within the entrance is seen a naked old man who is a Guardian of the Threshold. Three figures approach the entrance seeking initiation. The one on the left is blindfolded and awkwardly feels his or her way forward. Beside this person is another figure (possibly a woman) wearing a hat with a large, ostentatious feather plume,

1604

Mandala Sixteen.

which seems to have fallen over her eyes. She rests on one knee, being weighed down by a heavy purse. On the right, a third figure gestures, seemingly in amazement, at having found the entrance-way. In the center foreground, a hare or rabbit bolts into a burrow, and we are reminded of Steffan Michelspacher's Rosicrucian engraving of the Mountain of Initiation (see Mandala Group Six, plate 3) in which a rabbit or hare similarly appears. The date 1604, appearing on the right, is the symbolic date of the opening of the Tomb of Christian Rosenkreutz in the Rosicrucian legend. The Old Man looks towards the figure on the right. The two blindfolded travellers will probably not find their way to the Portal of Initiation. The Guardian of the Threshold sits upon a dead tree trunk and bars the way. If one satisfies this first guardian, one then passes through the gate down a passage leading into the mountain. This is the first test of the initiate. The Portal of the Guardian is flanked by the symbol of a hare on the left and a hen sitting upon eggs on the right. There are two ways of proceeding in the alchemical process of inner transformation: either by the nimble, active energies pictured as the hare, or through the slow, steady, patient brooding of the hen. Both facets must be cultivated in alchemy.

Having been made aware of these aspects of the work, the initiate can pass by the gatekeeper and follow the passage leading in and round to the left, where it emerges above, within piled up rocks guarded by a fiery dragon. Having passed the first Guardian and survived the passage through the inner darkness of the Mountain, we must encounter the dragon, a picture of the primal unresolved energies of our unconscious. If we have the inner strength to pass by the dragon, we are then able to stand upon a plateau in the center of the Mountain and peruse its mysteries.

At the center of this space, upon a large rock, stands a great Lion, barring our way to the next stage. At this point the initiate has gained a knowledge of the primal energies of his being, but has not yet integrated them. He must have the courage to face up to the Lion, which is a manifestation of the human soul. In a sense, this is a reflection of the egoism that can easily arise at this point, a false spiritual pride that is unwarranted and as yet unearned. But if we can conquer this tendency within ourselves, then we pass our third guardian, the Lion, and come to the door of the tower or inner citadel. There we will meet two soul birds, the Black Crow and the White Eagle. These soul birds enable us to experience different realms of our being. The Crow takes one down into the dark depths of the unconscious, while the White Eagle soars high into the spirit and flashes down with an essence of spiritual wisdom.

To the left of the Tower we see a wooden basin or tub with the Sun and Moon contained within. This image represents a purification through a washing of the solar and lunar facets of our nature. To the right, a purification through distillation in a flask set in a furnace is shown. Washing symbolizes purification from *outer* dross or accretions upon the soul, while distillation symbolizes an *inner* purification of the soul. We pass then through the inner portal and stand within the inner castellated sanctuary. On the right, the figure of an old man is planting a tree in the tub below. This living tree extracts through its roots an essence of the Sun and Moon forces from below and bears these as fruits in the seven-pointed star (representing planetary forces) and the flask. On the left, above the furnace, a tree bare of foliage has upon it three stars (Salt, Sulphur and Mercury) and it seems to lean over and absorb the smoke or essence rising from the distillation in the furnace.

On the heights of the inner sanctuary is the house of the holy spirit where the soul of the inner initiate might dwell and gaze down upon the world from the vantage point of spiritual awareness. On the peak of this inner realm is an orb with the sign of Vitriol ⊖ . This is also seen in another figure from the same manuscript, described in Mandala Seven, where it advises the seeker to "visit the interior of the earth and, by purifying, there discover the hidden stone." This orb can only be achieved, as we have seen, by the initiate who has undertaken this inner journey. As the goal of the journey, it has a crown above it signifying the spiritual rulership attained by those who reach this state.

MANDALA SEVENTEEN

The Mandala opposite is the frontispiece from Christianus Adolphus Baldinus' *Aurum Hermeticum* of 1675, and brings to our attention the central Hermetic maxim from the Emerald Tablet: "That which is above is as that which is below, and that which is below is as that which is above."

At the four corners of the engraving are seen figures representing the Elements: Fire and Air appear top left and right respectively; Earth and Water occupy the bottom left and right corners. These show the Gods and Goddesses of the Elements with their Elementary Nature Spirit inhabitants—the Salamanders of Fire, the Sylphs of Air, the Gnomes of Earth, and the Undines of Water.

Within the square of the Elements an oval space is seen. In the arc above we see the Sun, Moon and five planetary bodies, and the Latin word SURSUM, meaning 'upward.' The Sun has the upward pointing triangle △ (Fire), while the Moon has the downward pointing triangle ▽ (Water). These are also seen in an arc below the central oval space, in a kind of mirror image. In this arc is written the word DEORSUM meaning 'below,' alluding to the tenet "as above, so below."

This reciprocal balancing of separate upper and lower realms is fine in regard to the Cosmic Spheres. However, on the Earth the upper and lower planets meet in a more active, dynamic, union.

Hovering in the air, we see a winged disc bearing the interlaced triangles ✡ of the Sun and Moon above, from which rays descend. Below this, in a strange vessel filled with water, a shadowy image of this winged disc is seen. This is the mirrored inversion RETRORSUM of the upper winged disc. These are two realms within the soul of man, and the winged disc in the air represents that part of the soul that can reach up to the higher spiritual perceptions. This disc with ✡, showing the unity of the solar and lunar forces, acts as a link with the higher realm. The vessel with the water, however, represents a lower realm within the soul, closer to the material world of incarnation, that important region often disparagingly labeled the 'unconscious.' It is in this inner watery realm that spiritual impulses are truly digested, inwardly absorbed, and fixed into incarnation. We must therefore develop this inner image of the winged disc in our unconsciousness (like a photographic negative) so that this awareness can truly become a part of our soul.

To the right of the vessel we see a man with an axe in the process of cutting something in two. This action is labeled SEORSUM, 'apart,' a separated movement. This is the analytical facet of thinking which takes ideas and things to

Surfum
Retrorsum
Seorsum
AURUM AURÆ
Christiani Adolphi Balduini
AMSTELODAMI,
Apud Joannem Janssonium à Waesberge
Anno 1675
Deorsum

MANDALA SEVENTEEN.

pieces in order to find out how they work. On the left of the vessel is shown a bench with potted plants growing healthily. This is labeled HORSUM, an approaching or bringing of things together. This is the synthesis facet of human thinking, which unites ideas and perceptions of things in order to grasp their wholeness. The growing of plants is seen as an image of the bringing together of the Above and the Below in an harmonious manner. Behind the man with the axe on the right, we find a man turning a windlass at the top of a mineshaft, set upon hills which bear the ores of the planetary metals. These are the 'planets below' in the earth. The alchemist raises them and purifies them to unite the Above and the Below.

This mandala therefore refers to the alchemical union of opposites: as spiritual alchemists we must unite Above and Below, the left and right sides of our being (reflected, interestly enough, in the analytical and synthetic function of the brain hemispheres) within the inner vessel of the soul.

MANDALA EIGHTEEN

This mandala appears as an illustration in the 1682 edition of Jacob Boehme's *Signatura Rerum*.

At the top left and beside the mandala proper, we have SIGNATURA RERUM, the 'Signature of things,' shown in the form of a cross. Interestingly, on the vertical arm we see a polarity, in that on the upper limb SIGNA reads upwards, while on the lower limb TURA reads downwards. The letters 'V' and 'A' also incorporate a polarity.

Turning to the mandala itself, we see at the top a winged triangle bearing the fourfold Name of God, יהוה. It radiates seven rays or spiritual forces into the heights of the spiritual world. Below the central circular space of the mandala we see the Heavenly City, the New Jerusalem of the 21st chapter of *Revelations*, with the Lamb at the center and the twelve gates around it. Thus we have a polarity between God, remote in the spiritual world upon his throne with the seven spirits radiating out, and the establishment of the spiritual principles on the Earth as the Spiritual City. The mandala in the central space shows what must be integrated for these hidden, remote spiritual forces to be brought into outer manifestation as the realm of the Spiritual City.

This central mandala is surrounded by four flames, representing the spiritual archetypes of the four elements. These, added to the triune realm of the Divine, give the seven spirits. The Divine acts through the three parts of the Trinity—Father, Son and Holy Spirit—and also through the Quaternity of the Four Archangels of the Elements and Directions of Space (Michael, Uriel, Gabriel and Raphael, although they are not named here). These exist in the heights of the Spiritual World, but mediate through the zodiacal realm of the stars. Thus they connect with ♉ Bull, ♌ Lion, ♏ Eagle, ♒ Man. The twelve zodiacal signs in this middle sphere also relate to the twelve gates of the Heavenly Jerusalem. These four archetypes are further mediated into the central region of the world space of the mandala by the planetary spirits ♂, ♄, ♃, and ♀. Boehme calls the planets the Seven Properties and connects them with the Vision of the Godhead and with the seven candlesticks of Chapter One of Revelation. Boehme interprets the Seven Stars in this vision as spiritual principles externalized in the planetary bodies.

Above, at the top of the circular space of the mandala, a winged flaming triangle bears the Sun disc. This is the reflection of the upper spiritual triangle in the middle realm of the stars, the astral world. Below, polarized with this flaming triangle, is the square formed Cube bearing the lunar crescent. This is the Foundation Stone of the Heavenly Jerusalem, the Corner Stone of the

Christ. We note that it bears within it a shadowy, downward pointing triangle; we also note that the Sun disc above has twice fourfold radiating flames. The alchemist must unite the Three with the Four; that is, he must bring the spiritual Trinity into the material world of the Four Elements. These, when added together, form the Seven Principles; and, when multiplied, give the Twelve Zodiacal Gates of the New Jerusalem.

Moving out of these polarities, we realize that this mandala is dominated by a symbol which is not outwardly delineated. This is Mercurius ☿ , its planetary symbol being formed by the two wings of the Sun triangle, the inner central circle of the mandala, and the fourfold cross defined by the Cubic Stone. Mercury, the living substance of the human soul, unites the polarities, the spiritual and the material. We note also that the planets above the middle line of the mandala, ♂ and ♄ , have the cross of matter above; while the planets below this line, ♀ and ♃ , have the material cross below.

As alchemists using this mandala, we must place our consciousness at the central still point and, using the inner Mercury of our soul, unite the above and the below, the spiritual and the material, in order to contribute to the building of the New Jerusalem.

RERUM
VNGUS
TURA
יהוה

Mandala Eighteen.

MANDALA NINETEEN

This mandala, taken from Samuel Norton's *Mercurius Redivivus* of 1630, synthesizes the circular and tree aspects of Western mandalas that we have considered in a number of places in this book.

We see that this mandala is centered upon a tree, in fact, upon a rose bush. The roots are shown reaching below, while the flowers rise upwards from the central circular space of the mandala. This central space integrates the Three, the Four and the Two. In the outermost layer we have four circles in which three aspects are united. The outermost of these circles reads HYLE, the primal formless energy or substance of creation, and MENSTRUUM, the womb of form into which this primal energy was pressed giving rise to the Four Elements as a synthesis of these two. The next layer inwards shows us the ALBUS, or white lunar stage of the work; the RUBEUS, or red solar stage; and the NIGER or Nigredo, forming a similar triplicity, all of these being linked together as a whole, none existing without the others. Next we see three planetary God forms: VENUS, MARS, and JUPITER. Thus we have the masculine (Mars forces) and feminine (Venus forces) brought into balance by the law of Jupiter. The innermost circle shows three of the elements: Fire, Water and Earth.

Within this circle is constructed a triangle pointing with its vertex upward, and we can picture another triangle linking the other triplicities in the four outer circles, pointing vertex downwards. Thus we can trace the linking form of the seal of Solomon, the interlaced triangles ✡ . The upward pointing triangle integrates SPIRIT - SOUL - BODY, and Corpus, or body, is also here associated with the Saturnine realm, the dark *prima materia* out of which the spiritual emerges. Within this triangle is constructed a square, its four corners corresponding to the four elements, at whose center stands the figure of MERCURIUS, the Philosophical Mercury, balancing and uniting the polarities of the heavenly and the earthly, the Sun and the Moon, the masculine and the feminine.

This central mandala is placed upon the stem of the rose bush, linking together that which works below in the root realm of the dark earthly Saturnine forces, and that which points upwards to the heavens, the blossoms and the crown. Below, at the base of the roots, a toad (itself a symbol of the Saturnine dark realm of the *prima materia*) raises itself up from its normal prostrate position and begins to eat of the fruits of the vine growing round the rose bush. Two guardian Lions stand at the base of the stem.

There seems to be a definite link here with the Kabbalistic Tree of Life. This is not to imply that the creator of this picture necessarily worked out of a

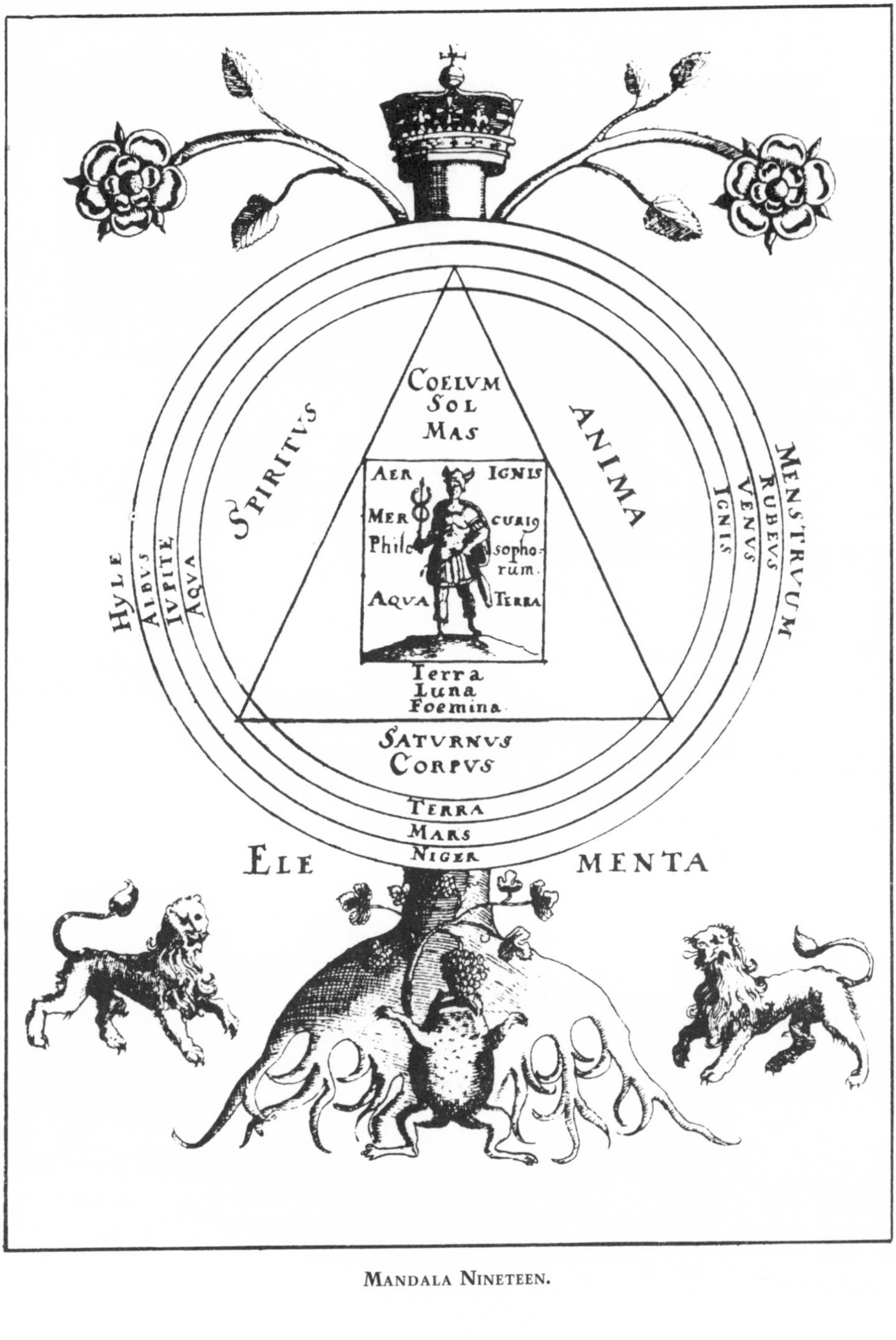
COELVM
SOL
MAS
SPIRITVS
ANIMA
AER
IGNIS
MER
CVRIO
Philo
sopho-
rum.
AQVA
TERRA
Terra
Luna
Foemina
SATVRNVS
CORPVS
HYLE
ALBVS
IVPITE
AQVA
MENSTRVVM
RVBEVS
VENVS
IGNIS
TERRA
MARS
NIGER
ELE
MENTA

Mandala Nineteen.

Kabbalistic tradition, but rather that he perceived the same archetypal structure in his view of the world. Thus the CROWN can be seen as the Sephira Kether, and the two roses, the red and the white, can be seen as Chokmah and Binah. The Mercury of the Philosophers is the linking element; it is the sap of the tree which rises and falls in the stem, ascending from the dark earth of the *prima materia* to its blossoming in the twin roses above. This Mercurius Philosophorum has a relationship to the Sephira Tiphereth on the Tree of Life diagram. The interlaced triangles can be seen as incorporating the other geometric elements on the Tree.

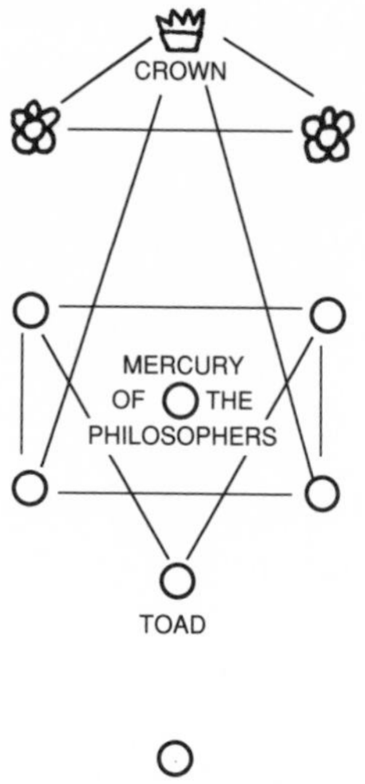
CROWN
MERCURY
OF THE
PHILOSOPHERS
TOAD

MANDALA TWENTY

This plate from Jacob Boehme's *Mysterium Magnum* seems at first to be a conventional 'Kabbalistic Tree of Life' diagram. As this can be explored quite easily by the reader, we will look here at the internal symmetries and correspondences worked out in the geometry of the mandala.

We will note immediately that it is centered upon the Christ and ties together the world of God (above in the radiating Sun) and humanity (set below in the ninefold rose). This central space of the mandala has a foursquare form, toward the top of which an upward pointing triangle leads to God, while from its base projects a downward pointing triangle.

This mandala integrates ideas connected with the sacraments. The central space ties together and unites various aspects of the sacraments in the central Christ. There are two polarities working: that of the upwards and downwards (spirit and matter), and that of the right/left (masculine/feminine, active/passive). Around the central Christ we have on a material level Bread and Wine, which has its spiritual correlation in the Flesh and Blood. The circle around this square also adds the correspondences of Bread (Vivification), Wine (Thanksgiving), Flesh (Remission of Sins), and Blood (Divine Union), these being four important facets of the sacraments. To the left we have the wheat plant (growing upon the realm of Nature) and, on the right, the Vine (set upon the realm of Earth). Both are receiving an impulse from above. The grain receives the heating rays of the Sun, while the vine receives a shower of rain. Grain can be seen, in this case, as the embodiment of the Fire element, and the Grape can be seen as embodying the principle of Water, and indeed we see these symbols set beside them. In the realm above, i.e., in the spheres of Grace and Heaven, they are embodied in the Sun and Moon respectively.

Thus this illustrator of Boehme—and I am not sure whether this can be ascribed to Gichtel or Freher—wishes us to picture the Christian sacraments as arising out of a meeting of two currents: one descending from above (Grace and Heaven), and ascending from below (Nature and Earth), through the two archetypal plants, the Grain and the Grape. On Earth these are the basis of Food and Drink but can become charged as sacraments with a spiritual power, nourishing the heart and soul.

The upward pointing triangle mirrors itself in the downward one. Thus on the upward triangle we have והי (mirror of יהו, Jehovah), while below we have אדם, Adam.

The upper triangle is centered on Faith, in the three dimensions as Spiritual Faith, Internal Faith and Supernatural Faith, linked by the three letters. The three arms of the Triangle bear two sets of terms:

Ascension into Heaven	Resurrection	New birth
From above	Eternal	Invisible

Below, in the downward pointing triangle centered on Sense, we have Bodily Sense, Natural Sense and External Sense, as the three facets connecting the letters of the name ADM. The three arms of the triangle bear:

Descension into Hell	Crucifixion	Old birth
From below	Temporal	Visible

The whole diagram indicates that "together all is one." This is set in a rectangular border in the corners of which we see the Cube of Earth, the Fivefold Rose of the Senses, the Cross of Faith, and the compass of directions symbolizing Heaven. These tie together the polarities of the realm of Grace and the realm of Nature. Boehme sees these realms uniting in the Sacraments, which come from the elements of Nature and the Earth, and yet become the vehicles for Grace and the Heavenly impress.

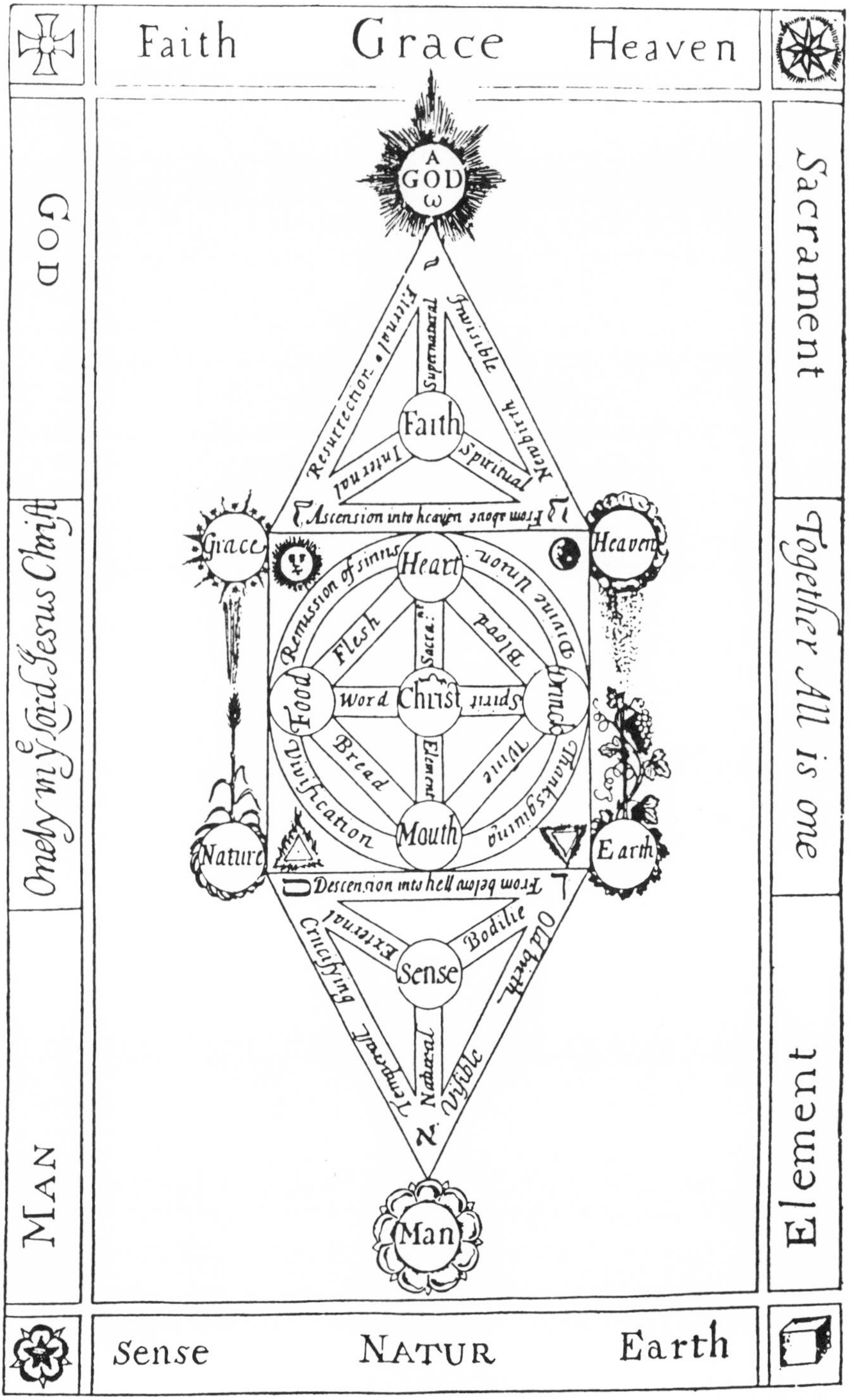

Faith
Grace
Heaven
GOD
Sacrament
Onely my Lord Jesus Christ
Together All is one
MAN
Element
Sense
NATUR
Earth
A
GOD
ω
Eternal
Supernatural
Invisible
Resurrection
Faith
Newbirth
Internal
Spiritual
Ascension into heaven
From above
Grace
Heaven
Heart
Remission of sinns
Divine Union
Flesh
Sacra.
Blood
Food
Word
Christ
Spirit
Drinck
Bread
Element
Wine
Vivification
Thanksgiving
Mouth
Nature
Earth
Descension into hell
From below
External
Bodilie
Crucifying
Sense
Old birth
Temporal
Natural
Visible
Man

Mandala Twenty.

MANDALA TWENTY-ONE

This illustration is found in a 15th century manuscript copy of a Lullist work on alchemy. This *Opera Chemica* is unlikely to have actually been written by Ramon Lull (Raymond Lully) (1253-1316), but is rather a pseudo-Lullist piece, written after his death by someone working in the spirit of Lullist thought.

Lullist writings are characterized by a systematization of philosophical and theological ideas using three basic diagrammatic forms: circular arrangements or WHEELS, divided into various segments, each bearing a letter and associated idea; TREES, in which the interrelationship of ideas is shown through branching diagrams in the form of trees; and LADDERS, in which the hierarchical structure of certain ideas is exhibited, each idea occupying a separate rung. These diagrammatic expositions of philosophy constitute the Lullist Art of Memory, a synthesizing of ideas into a whole, that can be grasped through a diagram as a totality. One can see quite clearly that later alchemical diagrams and illustrations from the 16th and 17th centuries often use a kind of Lullist framework as a skeleton for their design. Most of the early Lullist diagrams are entirely abstract, but the particular item here illustrated (which must be quite late) shows the evocative artistic use of images that one expects to find in Renaissance alchemical works. In its use of symbolism, it has gone beyond the purely abstract and into an imaginative use of symbols that speaks directly to the soul, and not just through abstraction to the mind. Diagrams such as these were meant to be worked with inwardly as meditative exercises and were not designed as mere illustrations or tabulations of abstract ideas.

This illustration is centered upon a tree, rooted in the earth. Its trunk grows through a vessel and has seven main branches, forming the habitation of a serpent. Around the branches of this tree are eight circles, and outside these a fourfold structure is created through four figures in the corners of the illustration.

At the top center of the illustration a Professor is seen in his chair, his banner declaring: "I am the teacher of Natural Science."

The four figures that surround the Tree make pronouncements about the Dragon-Serpent.

The Schoolman on the upper left declares: "Know that this Dragon never dies, except with his brother and sister."

The Schoolman on the upper right declares: "Know that this Dragon kills himself with his own dart, by swallowing his own sweat."

The King on the lower left declares: "I am the King, strong and powerful, and

Ego sum rerum naturaliū doctor

Mandala Twenty-One.

I fear nothing except that Dragon."

The young man on the lower right declares: "I am the naked man and the subtle beggar, of a strong nature, for I bear arms, and am made to kill the Dragon, and deliver you from fear and terror."

Thus we are pointed to the essential work of this process, the transformation of the Dragon-Serpent. This Serpent is the primal energy of the soul, the raw psychic energy, the inner potentialities of which so frightened the Patriarchs of the Judaeo-Christian tradition that they placed it in the Garden of Eden on the Tree as the Tempter. The alchemists, however, knew they could not deny the being, the essence, of the serpent within their souls; they had to encounter it, and come to terms with it, even though there were dangers to be met with on this path. (This serpent was recognized in other traditions, perhaps the best known being in Indian esotericism, where it is pictured as the Kundalini energies, the 'Serpent Power' in the soul.)

The Schoolmen point to the fact that the Serpent (*Kundalini*) does not die (i.e., become transformed) 'except with its brother and sister,' (the Pingala-solar and Ida-lunar streams within the soul, that parallel the Kundalini-Shushumna or central channel of energy). This Serpent-Dragon 'kills himself with his own dart,' and is transformed by its own inner forces 'by swallowing its own sweat,' by working upon and transmuting its own substance. The old King represents the hardened, fossilized mass of experiences and memories of the alchemist's soul that wishes to tackle the Serpent. The younger man is naked, not clothed with the past experiences that shackle the King facet, and thus he is that part of the soul which lives in the present moment as a 'subtle beggar.'

The illustration centers upon a tree growing upward, strongly rooted in the earth. It has seven main branches upon which are seen nine faces plus the triple-headed figure at the bottom of the trunk. These are the ten Sephiroth of the familiar Kabbalistic Tree of Life. (The Sephira Tiphereth is represented here slightly higher in the structure than is usual, but the geometry is obvious.) The heads are colored in various ways, one golden, another coppery, some being silvery, and some dark metallic grey. These are the seven planetary metals, the forces of Saturn, Mars, Venus, Mercury, Sun and Moon in the soul. Around the central trunk of the tree is entwined the green serpent, its head curling round the Sephira Kether, shown as the golden head of a woman, its tail reaching down to Yesod, shown as a silver-headed crowned man. These Sephiroth represent the subtle architecture of the soul, the inner structure of psyche, the balanced tree of forces that unites the upper and the lower, the heavenly and the earthly sides of the soul. These are united through three pillars or channels—Pingala, Ida and Shushumna channels, the solar, lunar and central currents of soul energy.

The Tree bears four legends inscribed on banners, one pointing upward the other downward. These signify the four archetypal levels on the Tree. From the top these read:

"After it has been put in the womb, and after the nuptials, the colors are green and citrine."

"It consigns it to death with its odor, so that it may dwell in life."

"He does not die, unless he appears dead."

"He who kills me and gives me my soul, shall rejoice with me for ever."

At the base of the trunk of the Tree is seen, in the position of the Sephira Malkuth, a triple-headed form, the central head being golden. From the necks of these three heads, three steams pour down, spiralling round the trunk of the Tree to flow into a grand vessel or chalice. This is the vast sea of the unconscious within us; the three streams represent the three archetypal links with the conscious side of our souls. In alchemy these are often characterized as the Salt, Sulphur and Mercury soul energies. SALT represents that tendency in the soul which leads towards the hardening, materializing, crystallizing and precipitating of soul impulses. The SULPHUR element is found in the outward radiating, fiery rush of soul enthusiasm toward some facet of the soul's life, bright energy darting here and there, mobile, reaching out and touching many things. The MERCURIAL archetype synthesizes and balances the Salt and Sulphur tendencies, making the constrictive element of Salt more mobile, and making the intangible nature of Sulphur more solid and fixed.

These three archetypal facets of psychic energy are found both in the conscious and the unconscious realms of the soul; indeed, they constantly move between the two. Thus a sulphurizing tendency in the soul toward some aspect of one's experience could arise either through a conscious decision or out of the unconscious realm, and this also applies to the other two of the Three Principles. They meet and flow together in the water of unconsciousness, in the chalice which holds the green, living soul substance. The three heads connect us with the Ida-Pingala-Shushumna psychic channels, and the heads on the right and left are nourishing two storks; the one on the left is golden and the one on the right has a silver color. These are a depiction of the Pingala and Ida Nadis or channels. Storks are known as birds that eat snakes, and this image has been used in the tradition of alchemical illustration. (See, for example, Matthieu Merian's engraved title page for Phillip Sidney's *Arcadia* of 1630.) Here these two soul birds of the solar and lunar forces keep the snake confined to the central channel, the channel of synthesis that is unpolarized and which indeed unites the two polarities. If the serpent-dragon were to find its way into the solar or lunar channels, a distorted rush of energy would flow through the soul and lead one into psychic problems and imbalance. Thus the storks are guardian figures, ready to eat up the snake forces if they intrude upon regions of the soul that they are not meant to occupy.

The branches of the tree are surrounded by an aura of seven circles, plus one inner circle. These correspond to the Ethers and Elements. The three outer circles (uncolored) correspond to the three Ethers. The next four circles moving inwards correspond to Fire, Air, Water and Earth. These bear the following legends:

Outermost Circle. "Observe that at the end of the tenth month, the spouse is ready, who is then born, a most generous king, wearing a diadem on his head. Therefore, take your king, coming from the fire, crowned with a diadem, and nourish him with his own milk, until he has attained his perfectly complete age and nature."

Second Circle. "And because he is prepared for begetting sons and creating daughters, to replenish the earth and see his sons and daughters to the first, second, third and fourth generation, know that these sons and daughters cannot perform remission except by pressing out blood and smearing ash, for there is no remission unless this is done."

Third Circle. "Pouring blood and sprinkling ash, this is the divine circle, and the names put down on the sacred page, the laws of life, and natural things over which I have power, emanated, we believe, from the Ineffable."

Red Circle. "This is indeed the Element of Fire."

Yellowish-Brown Circle. "Truly the Element of Air also performs much work, and unites to the men possessing it, so that in that Day, it goes forth in a strong and beautiful state."

Green Circle. "Now the Element of Water, when it has been well and truly prepared, in the way that you know, works wonders ...<damaged section of manuscript>... and regulates the lung."

Blue Circle. "Truly, the Element of Earth, when it has been separated and divided, divides everything, and is the treasure of the work, and drives off dross from the spittle and congeals Mercury."

Orange Circle. "There will be a great question (asked me by my friend), and he who has understood the great question clearly and well, shall have the Philosophers' Stone."

The alchemist must work through the seven realms of Ethers and Elements if the work is to proceed.

The two statements on the right and left, in proximity to the King and naked young man, perhaps sum up the interpretation outlined above:

On the left: "Let the reader observe the snake in the branches, next the three green living faces; let the skill of the worker who knows what he is doing hurry it thence into the hollow, in the form of drinking-water, desired by the thirsty, so that it unites the storks; this occurs when they have swallowed it. I have seen the three faces give way to a single product when they have been buried together, and when they have taken notice of each other in their hovel. So saying, let us proceed to fresh waters from the womb."

On the right: "The familiar group that are in the mountains are united in the tree, face to face, and look back to the highest heights when they have come down. (You will also obtain all the elements by these little-known means.) Their shape and form are in the mountains, but the portion in the sea helped them to become one. They have said with one voice that ants [sic] truly draw the four elements out."

The snake twining round the central three faces or Sephiroth in the upper soul must be brought down into the vessel of the lower soul. The three heads of the Three Principles flow together and 'give way to a single product' in the green living waters that pour through the chalice. The storks, the Ida and Pingala guardian figures, the solar and lunar forces, are united by swallowing the substance of the transformed Serpent-Dragon. The polarities in the soul—both horizontally, Male/Female, Yang/Yin, Right/Left, Sun/Moon, and vertically, Spirit/Matter, Heaven/Earth, Upper/Lower—are united together.

An illustration such as this reveals some of the profound insights into the architecture and energies of the soul which were an essential part of the Lullist esoteric stream, incarnated by Ramon Lull and worked through others into the 14th and 15th centuries. These insights provided a solid foundation for the symbolist tradition of alchemy.

The interpretation outlined above only touches upon one facet of the content of this illustration. Others, working from different perspectives, will find additional layers within its architecture, for its form, its symbolic structure, reflects an archetypal reality that can be approached from different angles and yet still remains true. Ramon Lull was indeed concerned with incarnating archetypal ideas in a structured form and this illustration certainly works in Lullist terms.

MANDALA TWENTY-TWO

This illustration by Freher, which is included in the William Law edition of Jacob Boehme's works, shows us the stages in the Creation of the World. Creation arises out of the Abyss, the groundless ocean of Being, which is

Nothing neither Darkness nor Light
Nothing neither Life nor Death
Nothing neither High nor Deep
Nothing neither moving nor stirring
Nothing neither seeking nor finding
Nothing neither place nor abode.

Within this resting ocean of Being, the first stirring is the recognition of the existence of the Byss or the Absolute Will to Be. Its qualities are

Will of the Abyss
Byss of the Deity of No Origin
Father of All Beings
Father of All Beginnings
The Unformed Power
Father of Eternity.

The Byss gazes into the Abyss, the Mirror of the Ultimate, and beholds his own being in this—not as Will, but as reflecting Wisdom, Eternal Imagination, the Infinite Mother. This is

The Eternal One without Nature and Creature
A Threefold thought but One only Breathing
Eye of the Abyss, Mirror of Wonders and All Wonder
The Outbreathed Mysterium without Nature.

From this Thesis-Antithesis-Synthesis arises the initial stage of Creation, pictured as the globe at the top center of the figure. Here the upward pointing triangle of Spirit and downward pointing triangle of Form are still intertwined. At their center, as a womb, lies the female Sophia-Wisdom element, while at the periphery, the male Adonai-Will forces hold their place. From this world of insubstantiality and inner warmth (temperature), two impressions are taken, which arise from the separation of the two Ternaries. The first is the

BYSS AND ABYSS · NOTHING AND ALL · TIME AND ETERNITY.
Eternity and Time when they agree, in Union joind and Harmony.
NOTHING NEITHER HIGH NOR DEEP.
FATHER OF ALL BEINGS
NOTHING NEITHER MOVING NOR STIRRING.
FATHER OF ALL BEGINNINGS
NOTHING NEITHER LIFE NOR DEATH.
NOTHING NEITHER SEEKING NOR FINDING.
THE UNFORMED POWER.
ETERNAL NATURE
SECOND IMPRESSION
FIRST IMPRESSION
NOTHING
JE HO VA
SHINING
FIRE
NOTHING NEITHER PLACE NOR ABODE
NOTHING NEITHER NESS NOR LIGHT
OUT BREATHE
SOLAR WORLD
EXHALATION FROM SPIRIT AND SPIRIT WHICH IS CALLED TIME IN TRIFFE OF VANITY
HIC EXILIUM, IBI PATRIA! ET INTUS BONA PULCHRA LATENT, IMO PATENT.
VANA VANIS! TERRESTRIA TERRENIS, NOS AS SURSAMUS ET EMIORE MUS

Mandala Twenty-Two.

Dark Negative Ternary, "an unsatisfied hunger and an anxiously eager restlessness," says Boehme. The second is the Light Ternary "in which Nature has surrendered its independence and is transfigured into the Light, in order for the fashioning of the Eternal Harmonies."

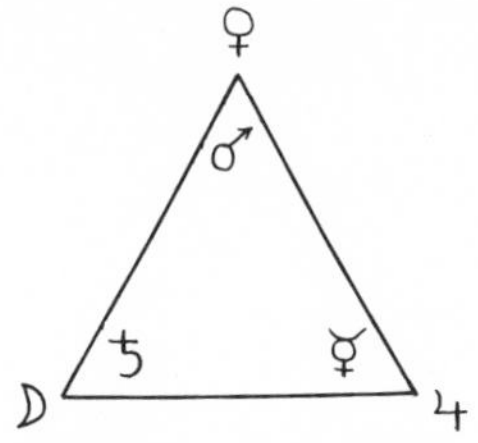
♀
♂
♄
☿
☽
♃

Upward pointing Triangle
of Dark World
♀ ☽ ♃ outwards; ☿ ♄ ☿ inwards

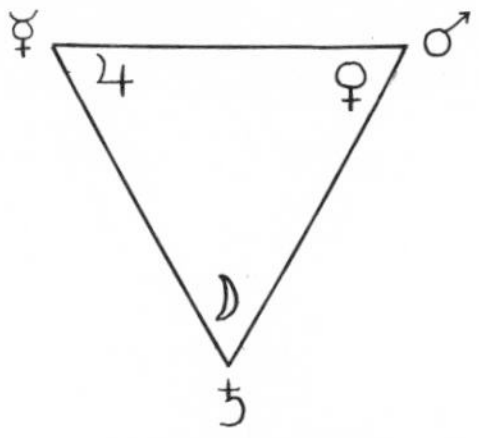
☿
♃
♀
♂
☽
♄

Downward pointing Triangle
of Light World
☿ ♂ ♄ outwards; ♃ ♀ ☽ inwards

Thus are born the Seven Principles which are associated by Boehme with the Planets:

♄ Contraction	☽ Form
♃ Expansion	☿ Inner Intelligence
♂ Circulation	♀ Love

The Sun ☉ arises at the meeting point of these two, the Light and the Dark Ternaries, in the Lightning Flash, the Shining Fire, the Twofold Fire that is both Wrath and Love, the Creative spark that is the Son (Filius), shown at the center of the illustration. From this arises the Cosmos as we know it, shown as the celestial globe centered upon the Sun with the Earth planet at the bottom center. This Solar World is the outbreathed exhalation from Spirit △ and Spirit ▽ which is called Time in Strife of Vanity.

MANDALA TWENTY-THREE

This 16th-17th century magical diagram, which is the record of a ritual working, gives us a glimpse into the consciousness of practicing ceremonial magicians, and provides a link between their workings with magic circles and the mandala tradition.

Adverse propaganda and negative superstitious prejudices have combined to paint a picture in most people's minds of horrific, abominable ceremonies and atrocious, barbaric practices being used by ceremonial magicians in their conjurations. However, here we have an example which should help to dispel some of these disturbed imaginings. Behind this ritual text we find a pure, highly spiritual individual, who sought to make contact with the divine, spiritual realm through his ceremonial magic.

This magical diagram or mandala consists of a triple circle, surrounded or sealed at the four quarters by four sigils in circular form. These bear a relationship in structure to the pentacles from the Greater Key of Solomon. The outer ring of the triple concentric circles contains a sevenfold spiral text, which is a petition to the Divine in all its manifestations for help in the work of contacting and binding spirits. This is a powerful invocation of fourteen Names of God (twice the seven spirals of the text), and the Archangels and Angels, for help in the task of 'subduing or binding' the spirit, or rather perhaps as we should now see it, of entering consciously into the spiritual world:

> O Father of Heaven, One God in Substance and Three in Persons, who suffered Adam and Eve, me and more to sin, and thyself to be crucified for our sins, I ask and beseech thee by all suppliant means and by the virtue of thy most holy names
>
> Tetragrammaton: יהוה
> Iah: יה
> Iava: יאוא
> Esch: אש
> Eheie: אהיה
> Iod Tetragrammaton: י יהוה
> Tetragrammaton Elohim: יהוה אלהים
> El: אל
> Elohim Gibor: אלהים גיבר
> Eloah: אלוה
> Tetragrammaton Sabaoth: יהוה צבאוה
> Elohim Sabaoth: אלהים צבאות

Sadai: שדי
Agla: אגלא
and by thy most reverent name Ihesus,
that thou would permit this spirit here appeared within this circle to show himself visibly to my sight, firmly to be here bound and neither to depart nor alter his personal appearance till I shall command him, but truly to perform whatsoever I shall command him without any hurt to my person or any of thy creatures, by the virtue of thy omnipotent power, through thy holy names, numbers and characters here composed, because thou hast said that in the virtue of stones, herbs and by the virtue of thy most holy names, thou givest power of binding and loosening of spirits by thy wonderful omnipotency Amen (אמן).

O High Deity and most merciful Father have mercy upon me, albeit I am truly thy servant, clarify my mind Oh Lord, with the splendor of thy heavenly wisdom and grant me a firm faith whereby I may subdue this spirit here appeared and so dignify this present circle with thy heavenly power and strength, that it may be a firm and sure bond whereby to bind this spirit here appeared, to hold his obedience truly to the present caller by the virtue of thy most high mysteries, and the power of thy mighty and potent intelligences, with thy celestial and elemental creatures, and that this present caller may by thy divine power through the virtue of this circle be defended from the malaise of this spirit here appeared:

Eternal God as thou givest power to the Archangel Michael, to subdue the proud and rebellious Lucifer, and didst grant power to thy apostles of binding and loosening of Spirits, and as thou didst promise to give the like power to all that should faithfully call in thy names, so grant this bequest, reveal now and evermore the strength of thy left arm, through the power of thy mighty Angel Camiel, by virtue of thy most powerful name Elohim Gibor, through this magnificent number Geburah, together with the virtue of the omnipotent name Tetragrammaton Sabaoth, by the power of thy potent Angel Hanael, with this victorious number Ha Sambroth, the power of all other administering Angels: and grant me, Oh Lord, thy humble servant, the caller of this spirit, ever more thy grace with undoubted faith and always mercy, by the power of thy right arm hand, through the virtue of thy all powerful name El (אל) by the assistance of thy most comfortable Angel Zadkiel, through the virtue of this most merciful number Hased In nomine Jhesu Amen אמן.

TE
TRA
GRAM
MA
NOT

Mandala Twenty-Three.

The next ring of the circle has a tenfold inward spiralling text which is addressed to the spirit that is being invoked. The petitioner commands the spirit to be bound by the thirteen Names of God, by the virtue of the inner connection between the soul of the caller and the spiritual realm. This petition is a statement of the stage of consciousness of the magician, as he lists the various aspects of the spiritual of which he has awareness, and through this awareness he has a greater inner strength than the spirit he calls before him. We can thus see in this, quite clearly, that the magician has become aware perhaps through a long period of training and preparation, of the architecture of the spiritual world. He now seeks, through a controlled spiritual vision, to have a direct encounter in consciousness with the spiritual world. This is not a magical operation of selfish power, but an open searching for direct spiritual experience:

In the names of the Eternal living and omnipotent God—יהוה
Agla: אגלא
Iah: יה
Iava: יאוא
Eheie: אהיה
Iod Tetragrammaton: י יהוה
Tetragrammaton Elohim: יהוה אלהים
Elohim Gibor: אלהים גיבר
Eloah: אלוה
Tetragrammaton Sabaoth: יהוה צבאות
Elohim Sabaoth: אלהים צבאוה
Sadai: שדי
Adonai Meleck: אדני

thou spirit here appeared within this circle by the virtue of me the caller, a creature and the Image of God, by the virtue of this bond, prayer and holy characters, be thou here constrained in the name of the Father, Son and Holy Ghost, to remain visibly and really in a fair form and not depart until I shall licence thee, and to answer and obey me truly and readily whatsoever I shall command thee, without hurting me or any of God's creatures directly or indirectly, without deluding any of my senses, and hereunto be thou bound by the eternal God to whom the fraternity of all living creatures hath belongest, at whose going forth the Angels are dropped down, the earth it opened and the depths are shaken.

Be thou bound by the true lion of the tribe of Judah who hath broken down thee and thy power: by that blessed body wherein the fulness of deity doth corporeally habit by the incarnation of our Lord and Saviour Ihesus Christe by his birth and miracles: by his mystical and most powerful sacrament, by his descension into Hell and overcoming death: by his resurrection and glorious ascension: by his triumphant coming in the clouds when he shall judge all according to their works.

By the seven most perfect gifts of the Holy Ghost whereso Ihesus Christ hath endured, and by the virtue of all the hidden mysteries of human redemption, and by all the powers and virtues contained in individual dignity, by the virtue of all these glorious names be thou here bound in nomine Ihesu אמנ: be thou here bound by the seven Celestial forces contained in the Intellectual Heavens, by all Intelligences and Presidents of all Celestial acts and their virtues, by all the holy orders and Hierarchies of Angels and Blessed Saints, be thou here bound by the virtues of Melachim to whom power is given to bind thy kings in chains and your nobles in chains of iron; be thou bound by all the fixed stars and their virtues, by the seven wandering planets and their influences and by all the heavenly numbers, figures and characters bearing force: be thou bound by the four elements and by the power of all virtues proceeding from the creatures commixt thereof. I say, be thou here bound by the virtue of all Infernal powers and their insufferable pains which here are immediately to be afflicted upon thee a thousandfold until thou be truly obedient unto me thy caller in nomine Ihesu.

Fiat + Fiat + Fiat + Amen + Amen + Amen.

The third innermost ring has the names of the Sephiroth in Hebrew.

In the center of this diagram a large triangle is drawn such that its vertices touch on the boundary of the first ring of text. The sides of the triangle contain nine names of the Archangels of the Sephiroth, from Metatron to Gabriel, leaving out the Archangel of Malkuth.

Within the angles of the triangle are three circles each containing symbols of the four-, six- and seven-pointed stars. The fourfold star has the names of the Angels of the four elements—Tharsis, Sorath, Ariel and Kerub—around the central Tetragrammaton. The six-pointed star has 'Adonai' written within it, and the seven-pointed star has 'Ararita.'

Inscribed in the triangle is a circle with eight names of God, and finally within this circle the pentangle with Tetragrammaton in its angles, and at its center a circle with inverted triangle.

This magical diagram thus bears within it the record of a ritual working, which is in itself the distillation of the Western magical tradition.

The four outer circles are the point of entry, the point of contact with the mundane world, the four directions of space and the four elements. The magician's consciousness stands firmly in the physical mundane world, but when he erects these four sigils he begins to open a door into the higher realms of his being. He then must step into the world of the soul. In consciousness he follows the first spiralling text inward through its seven circlings, calling on the different names of God, invoking a contact with the spiritual. At the close of this first immersion he touches upon the outer vertices of the Triangle. He has been led from the outer fourfoldness of the mundane world to a first perception of the threefold inner world. But he must penetrate deeper to a full awareness of this second circling. Down through ten circles, he experiences his inner wholeness, the integration of his soul, that has been achieved through previous spiritual work. Because of this, he stands inwardly strong enough to enter the spiritual world, to 'bind the spirit,' to have and hold a true encounter with the spiritual world in wide awake, everyday consciousness. Finally, the third and last circle is entered—that of the Sephiroth.

Then, having traversed the threefold circlings of the soul, he enters the spiritual within the central Triangle.

There he finds the nine orders of Archangels connected with the Sephiroth, excepting Malkuth, of which humanity is in essence the representative spirit. He experiences the spirits behind the four elements, and within the sixfoldness and sevenfoldness, and finally within the pentagram, he connects with the spiritual archetype of the Microcosm: Man the Pentagram, immersed in the four lettered Name of God, the Tetragrammaton.

Thus we find in this diagram not some horrific, ugly, fearful ceremony, but the record of a very pure and spiritual working. It shows a path, a quest for spiritual enlightenment, in the form of a magical mandala.

MANDALA TWENTY-FOUR

This mandala from the Altona *Geheime Figuren,The Secret Symbols of the Rosicrucians,* is an elaborate synthesis of alchemical and Christian symbols probably deriving from the Boehmist tradition. I have already commented upon another plate from this source (see Mandala Fifteen). In the original plate and the Aries Press translation the layout is rather cluttered, so I have redrawn the mandala and separated the text from the diagram. I hope this will allow us to see more clearly the structure of the mandala.

The top section shows the Virgin Sophia, the Eternal Feminine Wisdom Principle. On her right arm is written "Out of Eternity comes forth the crucified," which doubtless refers to the Christ child she bears within her womb. We are further told "Man know thyself and then you will know this figure." The child in her womb is nourished by two streams from her breasts. However, these two streams also pour down towards the lower world where they further polarize into the four spheres: Water, Blood, White and Red. At this point there is a kind of threshold. All above this point belongs to the spiritually potential, but all below lies in the realm of the outwardly manifest. Thus the four spheres of spiritual potentiality are mirrored in the four elements. From the center point Nature manifests herself as the divine instrument. Above we have Virgin Wisdom, below Mother Nature.

The Christ that is growing in the womb of Virgin Nature can be interpreted here in the cosmic sense, rather than in terms of the Jesus of the Gospel. The crucifixion of the Christ is seen as the descent of the Logos into the material realm, via the four elemental arms of the Cross of Nature. This reflects the mystical idea that humanity represents the Spirit crucified on the Cross of Matter.

In the lower part of this figure lines drawn from the spheres of the four elements lead us toward the central CHAOS. Hence the archetypal elements meet together in a chaotic interflow of substance that constitutes our material sphere of embodiment on the earth. Around this center we note "So was the world created / So passes away the glory of the world." Perhaps this is a reference to the genesis of the Earth globe, precipitating from the spiritual realm, and its subsequent passing away or dissolving back into the spiritual realm at the end of the world. Between the four archetypal spheres of the elements and this central point of chaos are three concentric circles with 12, 8 and 4 spheres respectively placed upon them. This forms a mandala picturing an integration of these elements through alchemical processes and symbolism.

We note especially the spheres which lie upon the central line connecting the Divine Instrument of Nature and the central chaos. The outermost of these is the Masculine Seed of the World; the Form of the Father pictured as a solar emanation. This meets the feminine Matter of the Mother, lunar in form, and we note a flow of forces being interchanged which results in the feminine being pregnant with the Sun and Moon children. These cosmic forces become mirrored on a still lower level, the sexuality of humanity, which is the Mechanism of the World. We also see a reference to the Golden River of Paradise, which is the Philosophers' Fountain. Four Elemental Waters (Rivers of Paradise) grow from one root. If we are able to set up within the structure of our souls a dynamic interconnection and balanced relationship of the masculine and feminine, we then gain power over the four elemental currents of forces within our beings. We are thus able to freely incarnate our spiritual intuitions in outer actions.

Let us look at the way in which these concentric circles form individual mandalas of alchemical ideas and processes.

The outermost circle is twelvefold with a left/right polarity. The top three spheres are especially linked by line with the threshold of the spiritual and material—the Masculine Seed of the world which we have looked at is in the center, the First Matter is on the right, and the Ultimate Matter is on the left. Thus we have moving downwards:

MASCULINE SEED OF THE WORLD

FIRST MATTER	ULTIMATE MATTER
The Closed Door of the Philosophers	The Way and Key of the Philosophers
Raising the Dead Dust and Ashes	Caput Mortuum Let there be Light
Gold of the Philosophers	Silver of the Philosophers
THEORY Philosopher	PRACTICE Magus

STONE

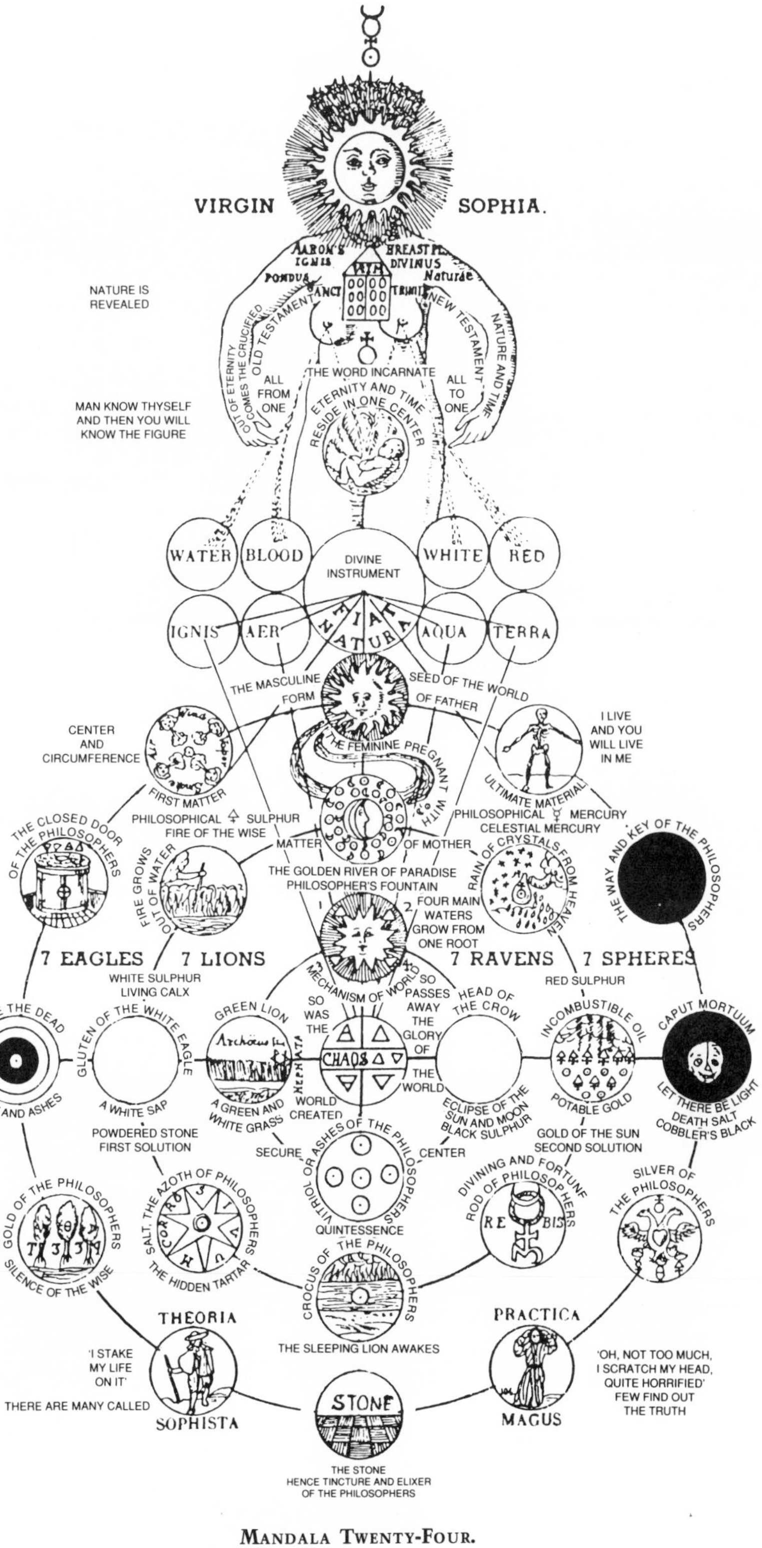
VIRGIN
SOPHIA.
NATURE IS REVEALED
MAN KNOW THYSELF AND THEN YOU WILL KNOW THE FIGURE
OUT OF ETERNITY COMES THE CRUCIFIED
OLD TESTAMENT
NEW TESTAMENT
NATURE AND TIME
ALL FROM ONE
ALL TO ONE
THE WORD INCARNATE
ETERNITY AND TIME RESIDE IN ONE CENTER
WATER
BLOOD
DIVINE INSTRUMENT
WHITE
RED
IGNIS
AER
FIAT NATURA
AQUA
TERRA
THE MASCULINE FORM
SEED OF THE WORLD OF FATHER
CENTER AND CIRCUMFERENCE
FIRST MATTER
THE FEMININE PREGNANT WITH MATTER OF MOTHER
I LIVE AND YOU WILL LIVE IN ME
ULTIMATE MATERIAL
PHILOSOPHICAL SULPHUR FIRE OF THE WISE
PHILOSOPHICAL MERCURY CELESTIAL MERCURY
THE CLOSED DOOR OF THE PHILOSOPHERS
FIRE GROWS OUT OF WATER
THE GOLDEN RIVER OF PARADISE PHILOSOPHER'S FOUNTAIN
FOUR MAIN WATERS GROW FROM ONE ROOT
RAIN OF CRYSTALS FROM HEAVEN
THE WAY AND KEY OF THE PHILOSOPHERS
7 EAGLES
7 LIONS
7 RAVENS
7 SPHERES
WHITE SULPHUR LIVING CALX
MECHANISM OF WORLD
RED SULPHUR
RAISE THE DEAD
DUST AND ASHES
GLUTEN OF THE WHITE EAGLE
A WHITE SAP
GREEN LION
A GREEN AND WHITE GRASS
SO WAS THE WORLD CREATED
CHAOS
SO PASSES AWAY THE GLORY OF THE WORLD
HEAD OF THE CROW
ECLIPSE OF THE SUN AND MOON BLACK SULPHUR
INCOMBUSTIBLE OIL
POTABLE GOLD
CAPUT MORTUUM
LET THERE BE LIGHT DEATH SALT COBBLER'S BLACK
POWDERED STONE FIRST SOLUTION
SECURE
VITRIOL OR ASHES OF THE PHILOSOPHERS
CENTER
GOLD OF THE SUN SECOND SOLUTION
QUINTESSENCE
GOLD OF THE PHILOSOPHERS
SILENCE OF THE WISE
SALT, THE AZOTH OF PHILOSOPHERS
THE HIDDEN TARTAR
DIVINING AND FORTUNE ROD OF PHILOSOPHERS
REBIS
SILVER OF THE PHILOSOPHERS
CROCUS OF THE PHILOSOPHERS
THE SLEEPING LION AWAKES
THEORIA
'I STAKE MY LIFE ON IT'
THERE ARE MANY CALLED
SOPHISTA
PRACTICA
'OH, NOT TOO MUCH, I SCRATCH MY HEAD, QUITE HORRIFIED'
FEW FIND OUT THE TRUTH
MAGUS
STONE
THE STONE HENCE TINCTURE AND ELIXER OF THE PHILOSOPHERS

MANDALA TWENTY-FOUR.

At the bottom as a synthesis of the whole circle is the Stone, Tincture and Elixir of the Philosophers.

The Intermediate Circle has 8 stages, with left/right polarity, as is the case with the outermost circle:

MATTER OF MOTHER

Philosophical Sulphur	Philosophical Mercury
Fire of the Wise	Celestial Water
Fire out of water	Rain of crystals from heaven
White Sulphur	Red Sulphur
Living Calx	Incombustible Oil
Gluten of the White Eagle	Potabile Gold
Powdered Stone	Gold of the Sun
First Solution	Second Solution
Salt, the Azoth	Rebis, the Divining and
of the Philosophers	Fortune
The Hidden Tartar	Rod of the Philosophers

CROCUS (ASH) OF THE PHILOSOPHERS
The Sleeping Lion awakes

The Innermost Circle is grouped into two polarities:

THE PHILOSOPHICAL FOUNTAIN
Mechanism of the World

Green Lion	Head of the Crow
Archaeus	Eclipse of Sun and Moon
A green and white grass	Black Sulphur

VITRIOL OR ASHES OF THE PHILOSOPHERS
Quintessence

We see how the symbols in each of these spheres link them together in a system of polarities.

The outermost circle of 12 spheres outlines the spiritual principles behind the alchemical operations, in the relationship between the *prima materia* and the ultimate material, between theory and practice, and so on, while the intermediate circle of 8 spheres seems to describe the process in more explicitly alchemical terms, with references to processes and archetypal substances that the alchemist must obtain and use for this work. The central four spheres show the attainment of the end of the work: Creation, Head of the Crow, Quintessence, and Philosophical Fountain. These are four archetypal reflections of the aim of alchemical transformation.

Across the central area of the mandala is written:

7 EAGLES 7 LIONS 7 RAVENS 7 SPHERES

The Eagles correspond to Air
The Lions correspond to Fire
The Ravens correspond to Earth
The Spheres (globes) to Water (vessels)

This probably indicates that the process must be repeated sevenfold through each of the elements; that is, one must pass through the Eagle, Lion, Raven and Sphere stages seven times to achieve the end of the work.

There is a great deal of material woven into this symbolism, and this mandala could be interpreted in an ever deeper manner, where further interrelationships between the symbols would reveal themselves. However, the indications I have outlined here will provide a starting point from which the reader can follow this up in detail.

The following text is from the borders of the engraving:

(See next page.)

THE HEAVENLY AND EARTHLY EVE
MOTHER OF ALL CREATURES IN HEAVEN AND ON EARTH

GOD is an eternal, uncreated, infinite, supernatural, self-sustaining, heavenly and existing spirit, who hath become in the course of nature and time a visible, bodily, mortal man.

The DIVINE EYE through which God will see and create everything.
The beginning of everything predicts its end.

THE LIGHT OF GRACE
ERGON - THE GREATER WORK

THE HEAVENLY EVE
THE NEW BIRTH

O Man, O Man, contemplate how God, the eternal Word, became man.

Innocent I received.
Damned is he who does not believe.

THE HEAVENLY TINCTURE
The Sacrament of the Holy Spirit.

NATURE is a temporal, created, terminal, natural, essentially spiritual-corporeal spirit, an image, likeness and shadow, fashioned after the uncreated eternal spirit, hidden and yet visible.

The NATURAL EYE through which Nature sees and reigns over everything.
The living is mortal, corruptible and will be reborn again.

THE LIGHT OF NATURE
PARERGON - THE LESSER WORK

THE EARTHLY EVE
THE OLD BIRTH

O Man, O Man, contemplate how Nature is a great world and hath become man.

Innocent I give back.
Despise not thyself in shame.

THE PHYSICAL TINCTURE
Virgin's milk and sweat of the Sun,
mother of six children and a pure virgin.

ROSICRUCIAN PHILOSOPHERS

Come, come, come. Who has eyes to see, can and will see rightly.
Come, arouse, arouse the ears. Whoever hath ears to hear need not be called upon too loudly.

Seek the friendship of Archaeus, the trusty doorkeeper, for he hath sworn allegiance to Nature and is Nature's secret servant.

MANDALA TWENTY-FIVE

I have decided to depart somewhat from my usual convention of reproducing a woodcut, engraving or design from the Hermetic tradition, and instead focus on a painting by William Blake from 1821. This painting, known as the 'Arlington Court Painting' and only discovered quite recently, is a work of Blake's final years and, in a sense, encapsulates his view of the evolutionary progress of the human soul which he had outlined in his important prophetic poems *Milton*, *Urizen*, and *Jerusalem*. Blake, of course, had read his way into, and was familiar with, the Neoplatonism popularized by Thomas Taylor, the Kabbalah, and general Hermetic ideas. However, Blake preferred to create his own mythology and symbolic material in order to reflect his own spiritual insights, rather than slavishly adhering to existing systems. Therefore, if we wish to grasp Blake's intentions in depth, we must enter into his own system and try to discover what he intended by the various beings and forces he presented. For the purpose of this commentary, however, I do not intend to take this path. Rather, I intend to apply the same methods I have used before in looking at earlier Hermetic engravings, as this painting of Blake is so pure and archetypal that the symbols he uses transcend his own system and relate directly with the symbolic material of Hermeticism.

The title that Blake gave to this painting, if any, has not been recorded, but later commentators have called it 'Regeneration,' 'The Circle of the Life of Man,' and 'The Cave of the Nymphs,' among others. The painting is obviously divided horizontally into two areas on the left and the right, and vertically into three areas: an upper region, a middle realm and a lower region.

Let us look first at the left/right division. On the left side of the painting we see two figures in the middle ground upon the shore of a wild sea. The crouching male figure wears a red robe while his female companion is dressed in white. He makes a horizontal gesture outward, while his consort points her left hand heavenward and her right hand towards the earth. She seeks to unite the earthly and the heavenly, while he seems to be concerned with the dynamics of the polarities of the middle world, relating the wild unconsciousness of the sea realm with the solidity of consciousness, indicated by the land on which they stand. In alchemy these figures parallel the Red Man and his White Wife, who must be conjoined through the Great Work to create the red and white tinctures or stones.

Above them in the heavens, we see a chariot drawn by four white horses which are attended by four maidens. In this chariot a man sits in a nimbus of flame, but has fallen asleep. Musician spirits attend him, but their music does not awaken him. Immediately below these two central figures a man lies drowning in a sea of flames with three female figures helping him on his way. These are obviously that aspect of the triple feminine described in Greek mythology as the Three Fates—Clotho, Lachesis, and Atropos—for they hold the skein or thread of his life. Clotho holds the distaff, Lachesis measures the thread, and Atropos on the left holds the shears and is about to cut the thread. Out across the turbulent sea a naked female figure is being borne on the backs of four black horses, attended by a female and a male figure. Blake must have intended in this left side of the picture to show the existential state of our souls. For if we devote our souls entirely to the earthly realm we ultimately have to yield to the laws of Fate that apply to our outer bodily makeup, and through this facet we can only touch the transitory, ephemeral element of life. The male figure, drowning in the sea of fire, looks longingly at his soul partner climbing the steps to his right (we will look at this facet in a moment). High above in the spiritual world our souls are still unconscious, asleep to spiritual potentialities, as we have not yet developed the ability to remain conscious in the spiritual world. So Blake draws us to the true realm of human transformation, the inner world of the soul. This has two sides: There is the shifting, ever-mobile swell of the tempestuous sea of unconscious forces within our beings, upon which rides the female figure who portrays to us those inspirations and intuitions that come to us from this inner sea. On the other side there is dry land, the solid ground in our soul, upon which the two main figures can stand. The female element in the soul seeks a union of the above and the below, the spiritual and the material realms in which our souls are constantly immersed. The male side of the soul, on the other hand, seeks rather to still the turbulent waters within the soul and make a more stable connection with this realm, which is dangerous and yet holds out great promise of insight and intuitions.

On the right side of the painting we see an alternative view of the soul's progress, a more linear and less dynamic one. Here a flight of steps rises from a river or pool at the bottom right of the painting, through a grove of four trees set out like pillars, and continues to ascend up a mountain. At the top of the mountain is a grotto in which we see angel-like beings bearing vessels of water upon their heads. We see a female soul figure in a flaming robe just beginning her ascent of the steps, bearing her bucket drawn from the river or pool. Below her we see another who has failed in her task; she has fallen asleep with her bucket lying horizontally in the water. As the figure climbs the steps she meets, like her male counterpart seen in the flaming water to her left, three female figures of fate. They bear a net to snare and a cord to bind the soul. But in this case they seem to be about to let her pass by. When she rises higher she

MANDALA TWENTY-FIVE.

will meet another facet of the triple feminine, the three Graces who dance their joyful celebration of creative energy in the soul. If she learns to gain the essence of their impulse from them without becoming entirely caught up in their dance, the soul figure can bear her vessel of water further upward. The soul will then become winged through the spiritual insight, which she gains from bearing the waters of the lower soul into the heights within her being. Therefore the water is depicted as being borne above the head, and the intellect is thus portrayed as subsidiary to, and watered by, the inspiration of the spirit.

Thus Blake in this painting points out two paths that lead to the spiritualization of the soul and the uniting of the forces below with those above. In this sense the painting is deeply Hermetic in conception and parallels many of the mandalas we have looked at earlier in this volume.

MANDALA TWENTY-SIX

I have reproduced this mandala from a German manuscript which Manly Palmer Hall suggested has Rosicrucian connections in his *Codex Rosae Crucis*.

Symbolically it is centered on Mercury in its various forms. This primal mercury, arising out of the Dragon of Chaos, is metamorphosed through the central cross with Sun and Moon, in order to be resurrected as the living Mercury of the Philosophers, the vital force behind living things.

The Dragon or Demogorgon is triple-headed and can be seen as representing the raw energies of our unconscious selves, or as the powerful untamed chemical energies (in chemistry, affinity) found in raw, unpurified materials. This Dragon is part serpent, part bird—it is inherently earthly and yet bears within itself the potential to soar upward in the soul as a bird. In order for this metamorphosis to occur, the Dragon must sacrifice itself. As we see, it turns itself on its back, feet in the air and out of contact with the earth, and seizes its tail in one of its mouths. Here it begins to look not unlike an embryo developing in the egg. (This may be an image intended by the creator of this mandala, for we note that in the circular border around the central space reference is made to the outer fire and the inner fire: the outer fire is necessary to warm the egg, while the inner spark of life is necessary for the development of the embryo.)

Through adopting this 'Ouroboros posture,' the Dragon creates a space in the soul where its sacrificial gesture is reflected in the Cross of Christ. The Cross bears a Solar Disc and above it the horns of the Moon, thus forming the abstract symbol of Mercury, all of which is contained within the Ouroboros space.

The Cross is referred to as 'the Magical Antimony of the Kabbalistic Philosophers.' Alchemists were fascinated by Antimony. Although a poison, in homeopathic dilutions it was recognized as a powerful medicinal remedy. It is also a chemically paradoxical substance: on the one hand it has all the properties of a metal, while in other situations it appears as a non-metal. (Present day chemistry recognizes it as a metalloid, together with Arsenic, Gallium, Selenium, Germanium and a few others. Interestingly, one result of the ambivalent characteristics of these metalloids is that when deposited in thin films on silicon they can be used to create transistors and integrated circuit 'micro-chips.') It is perhaps this paradoxical nature of Antimony which made the designer of this mandala associate it with the cross that bridges the gap between the lower Dragon of dark Chaos and the spiritual realm of light and life—the Cross that is simultaneously a symbol of suffering and transcendence.

Above this space, and growing out of the Mercury symbol, are a rose and a lily, the archetypal forms of the Red and White Tinctures. They grow out of the darkness of the Dragon's realm, through the cross, and up towards the spiritual light.

Around the periphery are the seven familiar planetary archetypes and, outside this, fourteen symbols of common alchemical minerals, including Sal Ammoniac, Sulphur, Crocus Mars, Tartar, and Orpiment.

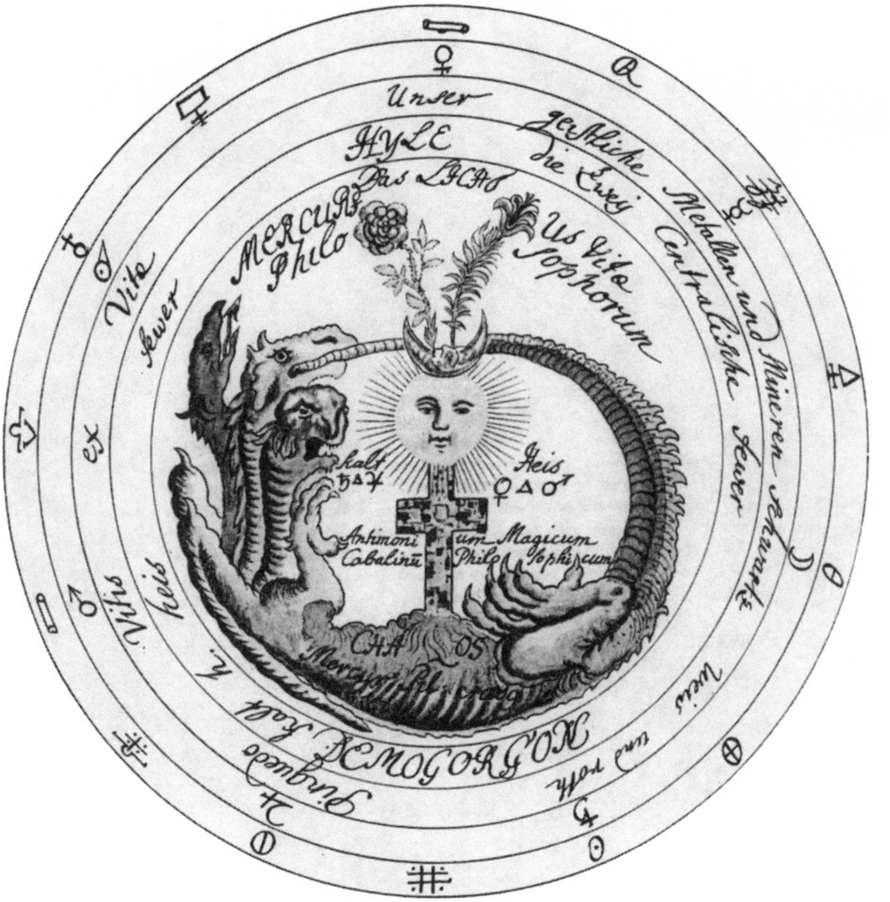
Unser
HYLE
MERCURI
Philo
Us vito
Sophorum
Vite
ex
Vitis
heis
kalt
Heis
Anthimoni
um Magicum
Philo Sophi cum
CHA OS
weis und roth
Feuer

Mandala Twenty-Six.

MANDALA TWENTY-SEVEN

This alchemical mandala, from a tract entitled "The All Wise Doorkeeper" contained in the *Musaeum Hermeticum* of 1625, does not require a lengthy commentary. It ties together the Four Elements, the four diagonal spokes of the wheel, with the seven spheres of the planets and the realm of the zodiacal constellations. The four cherubs blow their influences from the outer cosmic region toward the center, descending through the realms of the planetary spheres to the Earth globe at the center, which is the place of NATURE. The seven spheres are associated through the elements with different qualities: FIRE with the seven Angels, AIR with the seven organs of the human microcosm, WATER with the seven metals, and EARTH with the seven planetary bodies. The realm of Nature is threefold. There are Three Principles, Three Worlds, Three Ages, and Three Kingdoms in Nature. At the very center is pictured an individual soul with two guardian angel forms. The text round this says "It is the great honor of faithful souls that from their very birth an angel is appointed to preserve and keep each of them." Around this are shown the seven Liberal Arts and five Sciences through which humanity can strive for an understanding of the spiritual ground of the world.

This mandala summarizes the Hermetic conception of the place of humanity in the scheme of things, picturing in a neat and beautiful way the relationship between our human microcosm and the vast space of the macrocosm within which we live, and of which we are but a small part.

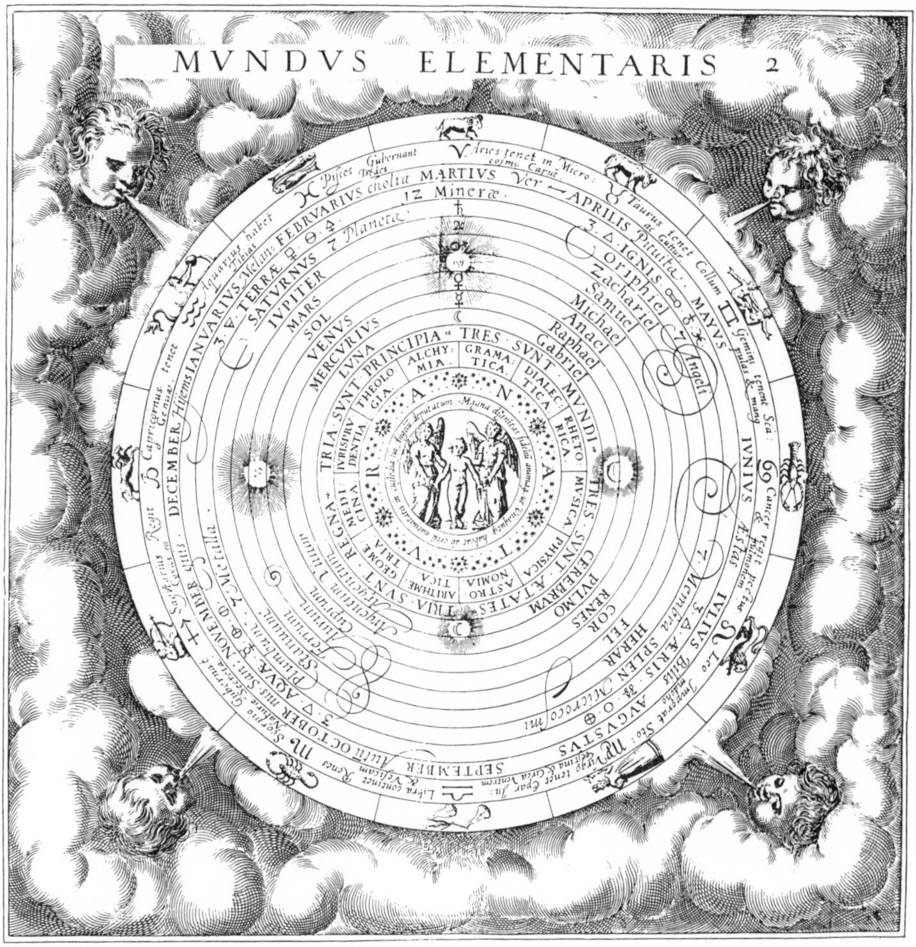
MVNDVS ELEMENTARIS 2
MARTIVS
APRILIS
MAYVS
IVNIVS
IVLIVS
AVGVSTVS
SEPTEMBER
OCTOBER
NOVEMBER
DECEMBER
IANVARIVS
FEBRVARIVS
SATVRNVS
IVPITER
MARS
SOL
VENVS
MERCVRIVS
LVNA
Oriphiel
Zachariel
Samuel
Michael
Anael
Raphael
Gabriel
TRIA SVNT PRINCIPIA TRES SVNT MVNDI
TRES SVNT ÆTATES
TRIA SVNT REGNA
THEOLO GIA
ALCHY MIA
GRAMA TICA
DIALEC TICA
RHETO RICA
MVSICA
PHYSICA
ASTRO NOMIA
ARITHME TICA
GEOME TRIA
MEDI CINA
IVRISPRV DENTIA
CEREBRVM
PVLMO
RENES
COR
FEL
SPLEN
HEPAR

Mandala Twenty-Seven.

MANDALA TWENTY-EIGHT

This is a beautiful though rather enigmatic mandala which appeared in 1600 as the title page to Beroalde de Verville's commentary to, and French translation of, the important Renaissance allegory*Hypnerotomachia* (or *The Dream of Poliphilus*).

The mandala is structured with eight main symbols at the corners and along the edges of a rectangular space. However, it is to be read from the bottom center, where the narrow branch or trunk of a tree is seen rising up and sending its branches to all the symbols of the mandala.

The symbol group at the bottom center is a circle representing the Chaos of the Four Elements and the symbols of the planetary forces. At the center of this sphere are symbols for Fire (flames) and Water (the drops). The whole mandala explores the path to the spirit experienced through the dynamics of the relationship of these two elements. We see a path leading from the flame/drop at the bottom center to the phoenix, or soul bird, rising towards the light, at the top center.

On the left of the Chaos sphere we see the paradox of a tree with a fire at its roots, fueling the flames by dropping its leaves. The path on the left leads on from this paradoxical tree that consumes itself, through the Ouroboros, in which a serpent and a winged dragon simultaneously consume each other. Beside them are the symbols for Mercury ☿ and Aqua Fortis 🜅 . If one places metallic Mercury in Aqua Fortis ('Strong Water' or concentrated nitric acid) each consumes the other; the Mercury dissolves into solution as mercuric nitrate and the strength of the acid is correspondingly reduced. Aqua Fortis or nitric acid was a paradox to the alchemists, being a water that fumed and burned. Mercury was also an enigma, a metal that is a liquid. Above this is a lion with its four paws removed. As a symbol it has been spiritualized by the removal of its direct contact with the earth and it also becomes a paradoxical symbol—the fierce lion without the means of manifesting its ferocity. In alchemy the Lion is sometimes associated with fire, and the blood (or watery part) of the Lion is often seen as a primal substance of the alchemical work. Also, the alchemical symbolism of the Green Lion sometimes represents the energies of Nature found in the sap of plants, and may here be related to the fruiting of the plant world symbolized in the cornucopia.

On the right hand side of this mandala, a path uniting fire and water seems to be outlined. Below, in the right corner, a wise man sits on a throne with the Sun at his feet and the Moon crescent symbol on his head. He holds a book, on the cover of which are seen alternating symbols of flames and water drops.

LE
TABLEAV
DES RICHES
INVENTIONS
Couuertes du voile des feintes
Amoureuses, qui sont re-
presentees dans le
SONGE DE POLIPHILE
Desvoilees des ombres du Songe,
& subtilement exposees
PAR BEROALDE
A. PARIS.
Chez MATTHIEV GVILLEMOT, au Palais,
en la gallerie des prisonniers.
Auec priuilege du Roy.

MANDALA TWENTY-EIGHT.

Above him a dragon with wings of fire and breathing flames is paradoxically able to swim on the open water. On the dead trunk of a tree a fountain is placed. Beside this a flame is seen warming the base and keeping the water circulating eternally. Alongside this is a water drop, and further to the left the seemingly dead trunk sends forth a new regenerating shoot. Above this is a cornucopia, representing the abundance of the fruits of nature that comes with the completion of the alchemical work. A single rose falls from the horn and drops five petals towards the flame and water drop on the tree trunk with its fountain and new growth. Beside the cornucopia is an hourglass which points to the fact that out of all these cyclic processes—the self consuming tree, the Ouroboros, and the circulating fountain on the regenerating tree trunk—a time is reached when the process comes to fruition.

This mandala seems to put before us for our contemplation the fact that the path to spiritual awareness through alchemy involves an encounter with the paradoxical. Those who are suited to the alchemical work must be able to incorporate paradox, and integrate this within their beings.

MANDALA TWENTY-NINE

There are two very interesting engravings contained in an alchemical medical work by Malachias Geiger, *Microcosmus Hypochondriacus*, Munich 1652. Although these engravings by Wolfgang Kilian are derived symbolically from Matthieu Merian's engraved plates "The All-Wise Doorkeeper" in the *Musaeum Hermeticum* of 1625 (one of which in turn was originally used in Daniel Mylius' *Opus Medico-Chemicum* of 1618), they are well executed and re-worked into a new conception.

The first emblem (number five in the *Microcosmus Hypochondriacus*) addresses itself to the chemical preparation of the potabile gold, the golden elixir. This mandala clearly illustrates the Hermetic conception of the cosmos; it shows the starry world above the clouds with the archetypes of the planets, the two angels pointing towards the Trinity: Jehovah the Father, the Lamb, and the Dove of the Spirit. Between the Angels we note "All from the One, All in the One, All through the One." The influences of this starry world emanate down to the earthly plane below. Under the Tree of Life stands a woman labeled Sapientia with the motto "Sapiens Dominabitur Astris"—"the stars will rule the wise." (Interestingly, this was the magical motto of the supposed Fraulein Sprengel, mentioned in the cipher manuscript of the Hermetic Order of the Golden Dawn, who was the adept transmitter of its rituals and Hermetic knowledge.)

The Tree of Life bears the seven metals and the twelve alchemical metalloids which also appear in the Merian plate (see Mandala Five for a detailed description of this). On each side of this tree are two mountains, the left with the Phoenix of Fire and Air, marking the Dry Way, and the right with the Eagle of Water and Earth, the Humid Way. These are also taken from Merian's work.

Below the fire mountain we see the alchemical birds—the Peacock, White Swan or Goose, and Black Crow—with the motto "I am the Black, the White, the Yellow and the Red." Between the Sophia-Wisdom figure, two hunters are seen killing a winged dragon or bird.

Atop the mountain of the 'humid way' on the right, a pelican is seen in the sacrificial act of feeding its young with its own blood. A tablet with the uniting of the three principles, Sulphur-Mercury-Salt, promises "A long, easy, healthy, life of glory and infinite riches." In a cave under this mountain we see the figures of the Sun and Moon (Sun with Lion, Moon with Lioness) approaching the alchemical laboratory, where they meet Mercury with his caduceus, winged helmet and sandals.

INVNO OMNIA
VENTORVM
ANNVS SOLARIS
ANNVS
STELLATVS
ARBOR
VITÆ
EMBLEMA 3
AVRI POTABILIS CHIMICE
PRÆPARATI

Mandala Twenty-Nine: Plate One.

PATER BONUM INFINITUM
LUMINIS GRATIÆ
DEVS
MESSIAS
HOMO
MVNDVS ARCHE TY PVS
IDEÆ
SERAPHIM
CHERVBIM
THRONI
Hierarchia Clasis Prima
VIRTVTES
ARCHANGELI
ANGELI
Hierarchia Clasis Tertia
DOMINATIONES
PRINCIPATVS
POTESTATES
Hierarchia Clasis Secunda
MVNDVS INTELLIGENTIARVM
MARTIVS Ver-
APRILIS Pituita
MAYVS
IVNIVS Æstas
IVLIVS
AVGVSTVS
SEPTEMBER Autum.
OCTOBER
NOVEMBER
DECEMBER Hyems
IANVARIVS Melan:
FEBRVARIVS
12 Mine
7 Planetæ
3. IGNIS.
3. TERRÆ.
3. AERIS.
3. AQVÆ.
7 Angeli
7 Metalla
7 Membra
SATVRNVS
IVPITER
MARS
SOL
VENVS
MERCVRIVS
LVNA
Oriphiel
Zachariel
Samuel
Michael
Anael
Raphael
Gabriel
TRIA SVNT PRINCIPIA
TRES SVNT MVNDI
TRES SVNT ÆTATES
TRIA SVNT REGNA
CEREBRVM
PVLMO
COR
RENES
FEL
HEPAR
SPLEN
Argentum Vivum
Cuprum
Aurum
Ferrum
Stannum
Plumbum
Microcosmi
MVNDVS ELEMENT ARIS
EMBLE MA. 4.

Mandala Twenty-Nine: Plate Two.

Through her motto, the Sophia figure under the tree suggests her awareness of the dimension of the Above, but she also gestures horizontally with her scepter towards the cave of alchemy, the spiritual work of the realm below.

The second plate is the fourth emblem from the *Microcosmicus Hypochondriacus*. It is almost an exact copy of the Merian plate from "The All-Wise Doorkeeper" (illustrated below), but is linked formally also with its sister emblem from the *Microcosmicus*. In this, emblem number four, the two angels gaze directly upward to the divine world of the archetypes, whereas in emblem five their gaze is outward, turned downward to the earthly realm. The globe below is the world of the elements and the Sphere of Nature, and it bears within itself a multiplicity of correspondences—the Planets, Angels, and human vital organs. It also bears on its circumference the zodiacal signs, with the months, four seasons and humors, while towards the center are the Liberal Arts, here expanded from seven to twelve to preserve the numerical correspondences.

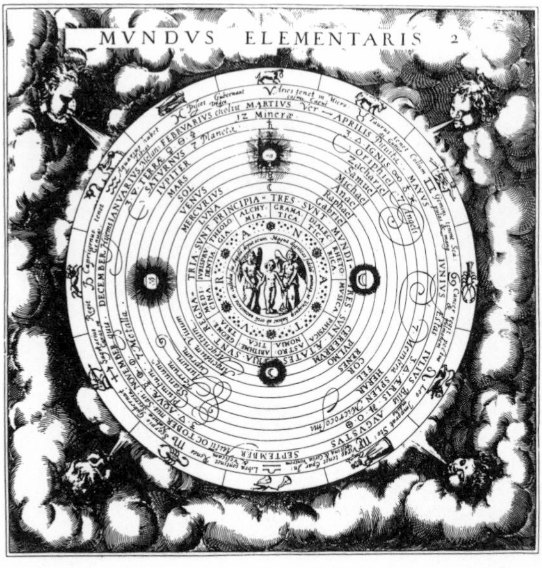
MVNDVS ELEMENTARIS 2

MANDALA THIRTY

This mandala appears as an illustration in the late nineteenth century writings of Eliphas Levi and, like many of the plates illustrating Levi's works, it is obviously drawn from the symbolism of the Hermetic tradition.

It has been described elsewhere as a plan of Solomon's Temple; however, this interpretation does not entirely withstand close scrutiny, for it is surely a Masonic-Rosicrucian emblem. The mandala is divided into three distinct areas, each of which has a cross: the area below, with the tower and pillar; the domain above, of the pelican surmounted by the Rosy Cross; and the middle region, which is found within a border reminiscent of the boundary forms of the yantras and mandalas of the Hindu and Buddhist tradition (for example, the Shri Yantra appears in such a border). This border is divided into 28 regions, representing the twenty-eight Mansions of the Moon: we further see the four phases of the Moon and the circle divided into 360 degrees. This is the circle of the zodiac with the twelve months (with their French and Hebrew names) which contains within a cross of the four elements. At the center of this cross is the eye in the triangle. The surrounding letters indicate the Universe or the World, and within this is drawn a sevenfold star. Also around this are the sacred initials I.N.R.I. (Iesus Nazarenus Rex Iudaeorum), sometimes interpreted in Rosicrucian circles as "Igne Natura Renovatur Integra" ("Nature is wholly regenerated by Fire").

Central to this mandala is a picture of the world seen as an interflow of the energies of the Moon and its four phases. The Moon mediates the light of the Sun to the world through its rhythmic phases, which continually cycle through the seasons of life: the waxing first quarter represents infancy; the full moon represents maturity; the waning third quarter represents old age; and the new moon represents death. A parallel is being drawn with the death-resurrection of Christ on the Cross, which is echoed above in the symbol of the pelican nourishing its seven young with its own blood. This is framed between the Rose and Lily.

It is tempting to interpret the tower and pillar as Joachin and Boaz, the pillars of the Solomonic Temple. However, the tower on the left is more like a medieval castle tower, while the pillar on the right is a more conventional picture of the Boaz pillar. Between these two is a circular figure bearing the word 'Immanuel' and a cross with a Rose at its center. This would seem to bear a reference to the 18th degree of the Ancient and Accepted Scottish Rite of Freemasonry, the Rose-Croix grade, with the symbol (in musical notation) of the admittance battery of seven knocks below. (This sevenfoldness is echoed in the sevenfold star and the seven chicks of the pelican.) Interestingly, in the Rose-Croix grade, the neophyte is at one point given the title 'Knight of the Pelican and Eagle,' and later is given the word I.N.R.I., which appears on various parts of this particular emblem. This mandala, therefore, seems to reflect the spiritual essence of the Rose-Croix ceremony of this particular form of Freemasonic working, which drew upon the Hermetic and Rosicrucian ideas in the structuring of its ritual.

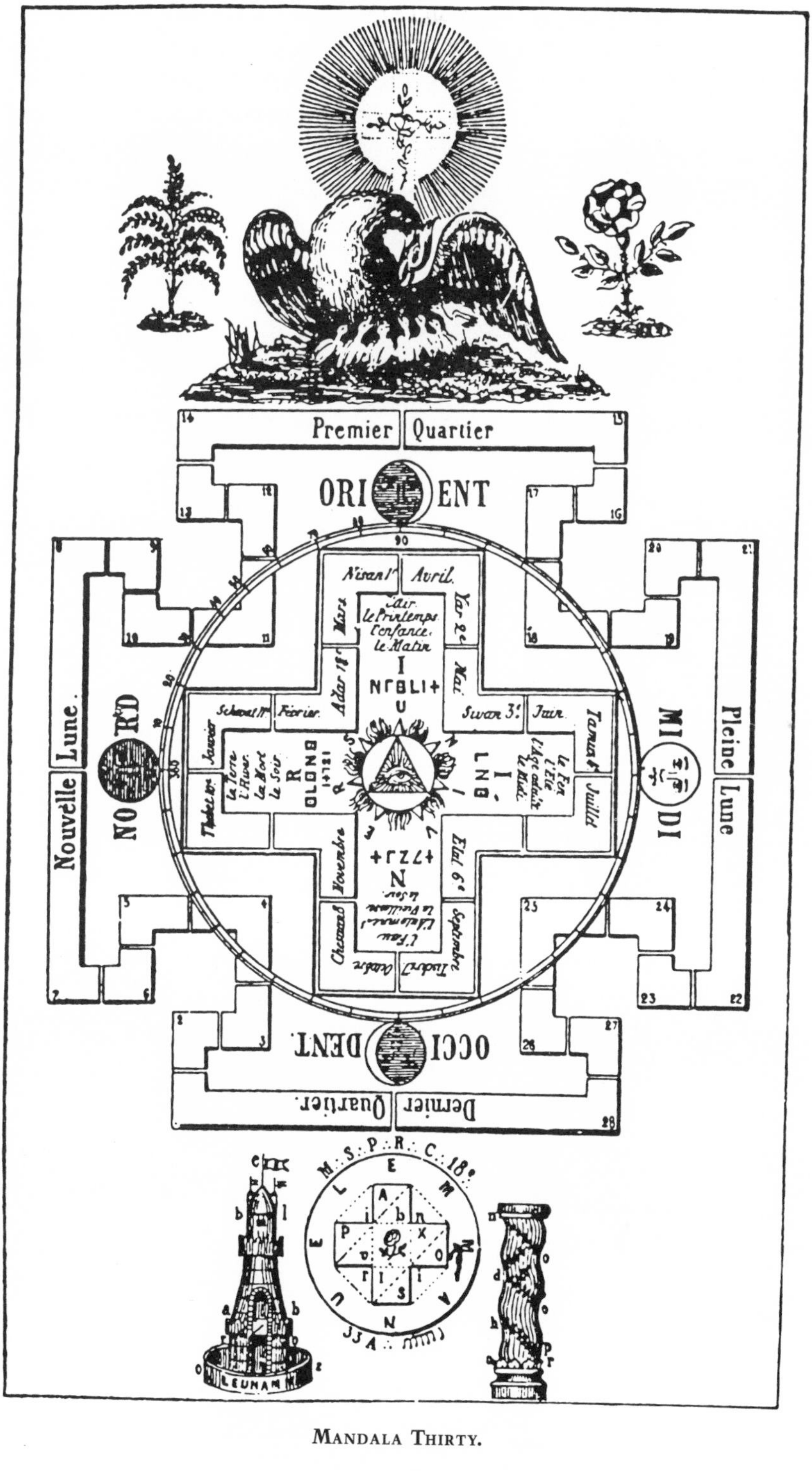
Premier
Quartier
ORI
ENT
Nouvelle
Lune.
NO
RD
MI
DI
Pleine
Lune
OCCI
DENT.
Dernier
Quartier.
Nisan 1er
Avril.
Mars
Yar 2e
Mai
Adar 12e
l'air.
le Printemps.
l'enfance.
le Matin
Schevat 11e
Février
Janvier
Thebet 10e
Siwan 3e
Juin
Tamuz 4e
Juillet
Elul 6e
Novembre
Septembre
Chesvan 8
Octobre
Tischri 7
le Feu
l'Été
l'âge adulte
le Midi.
la Terre
l'Hiver.
la Mort
le Soir
M.S.P.R.C. 18e
LEUMAN

Mandala Thirty.